TEACHER'S PET PUBLICATIONS

LITPLAN TEACHER PACK
for
The Chocolate War
based on the book by
Robert Cormier

Written by
Barbara M. Linde & Janine H. Sherman

© 1998 Teacher's Pet Publications
All Rights Reserved

This **LitPlan** for Robert Cormier's
The Chocolate War
has been brought to you by Teacher's Pet Publications, Inc.

Copyright Teacher's Pet Publications 1998

Only the student materials in this unit plan (such as worksheets, study questions, and tests) may be reproduced multiple times for use in the purchaser's classroom.

For any additional copyright questions,
contact Teacher's Pet Publications.

www.tpet.com

TABLE OF CONTENTS
The Chocolate War

Introduction	5
Unit Objectives	7
Unit Outline	9
Reading Assignment Sheet	8
Study Questions	13
Quiz/Study Questions (Multiple Choice)	21
Pre-Reading Vocabulary Worksheets	37
Lesson One (Introductory Lesson)	53
Writing Assignment 1	54
Writing Evaluation Form	55
Nonfiction Assignment Sheet	56
Writing Assignment 2	65
Oral Reading Form	72
Extra Writing Assignments/Discussion ?s	80
Writing Assignment 3	88
Project Ideas	90
Vocabulary Review Activities	92
Unit Review Activities	93
Unit Tests	99
Unit Resource Materials	133
Vocabulary Resource Materials	151

A FEW NOTES ABOUT THE AUTHOR
Robert Cormier

CORMIER, Robert (1925-   ). Robert Cormier was born and has always lived in Leominster, Massachusetts. He grew up there, went to school there, courted and married there, and raised four children in the house where he and his wife, Connie, still live. He never intends to live anywhere else claiming there are lots of untold stories right there on Main Street.

Cormier was a newspaper reporter and columnist for thirty years. He is inspired by news events, and in some cases, by circumstances in his own life, as the basis of his plots. He is known for his outstanding ability to create stories which capture human interest. He has an uncanny talent to make the reader see what motivates behavior which is often called evil, but becomes understandable when seen through the eyes of his characters. "I take real people and put them in extraordinary situations," he said in an interview in SCHOOL LIBRARY JOURNAL. Most often his themes involve intimidation and the way people manipulate other people, as well as the obvious abuse of power.

He began writing in the seventh grade. He says he can not remember a time when he wasn't trying to get something down on paper. He has been awarded many prizes for his controversial novels for young adults, including the Margaret A. Edwards Award of the Young Adult Services Division of the American Library Association. This award is presented in recognition of those authors who provide young adults with a window through which they can view the world and which will help them to grow and understand themselves and their role in society. He was especially thrilled with this award saying, " I've always hoped my novels could show adolescents the bigness of what's out there and that happy endings are not our birthright. You have to do something to make them happen."

Cormier loves to travel and has been to almost every state in the U.S. He also loves jazz, movies, and staying up late. Some other books written by this author include: *After the First Death* (1980), *I Am the Cheese* (1983), *The Bumblebee Flies Anyway* (1983), *Beyond the Chocolate War* (1985), and *Fade* (1988).

INTRODUCTION

This unit has been designed to develop students' reading, writing, thinking, and language skills through exercises and activities related to *The Chocolate War* by Robert Cormier. It includes twenty-three lessons supported by extra resource materials plus a class project.

The **introductory lesson** introduces students to background information about places, people, and events mentioned throughout this novel. It also doubles as the first writing assignment for the unit. Students are given time to research, write, and present their non-fiction information. After the presentations, students are given the materials they will be using during the unit.

The **reading assignments** are approximately thirty pages each; some are a little shorter while others are a little longer. Students have approximately 15 minutes of pre-reading work to do prior to each reading assignment. This pre-reading work involves reviewing the study questions for the assignment and doing some vocabulary work for ten to twelve vocabulary words they will encounter in their reading.

The **study guide questions** are fact-based questions; students can find the answers to these questions right in the text. These questions come in two formats: short answer or multiple choice. The best use of these materials is probably to use the short answer version of the questions as study guides for students (since answers will be more complete), and to use the multiple choice version for occasional quizzes. It might be a good idea to make transparencies of your answer keys for the overhead projector.

The **vocabulary work** is intended to enrich students' vocabularies as well as to aid in the students' understanding of the book. Prior to each reading assignment, students will complete a two-part worksheet for approximately ten to fifteen vocabulary words in the upcoming reading assignment. Part I focuses on students' use of general knowledge and contextual clues by giving the sentence in which the word appears in the text. Students are then to write down what they think the words mean based on the words' usage. Part II nails down the definitions of the words by giving students dictionary definitions of the words and having students match the words to the correct definitions based on the words' contextual usage. Students should then have an understanding of the words when they meet them in the text.

After each reading assignment, students will go back and formulate answers for the study guide questions. Discussion of these questions serves as a **review** of the most important events and ideas presented in the reading assignments.

After students complete extra discussion questions, there is a **vocabulary review** lesson which pulls together all of the fragmented vocabulary lists for the reading assignments and gives students a review of all of the words they have studied.

Following the reading of the book, two lessons are devoted to the **extra discussion questions/writing**

assignments/activities. These questions focus on interpretation, critical analysis and personal response, employing a variety of thinking skills and adding to the students' understanding of the novel. These questions are done as a **group activity**. Using the information they have acquired so far through individual work and class discussions, students get together to further examine the text and to brainstorm ideas relating to the themes of the novel.

The group activity is followed by a **reports and discussion/ activity** session in which the groups share their ideas about the book with the entire class; thus, the entire class gets exposed to many different ideas regarding the themes and events of the book.

There are three **writing assignments** in this unit, each with the purpose of informing, persuading, or having students express personal opinions. In Writing Assignment 1, writing to **inform**, students develop a report based on their non-fiction research. For Writing Assignment 2, **expressing a personal opinion**, students will be asked to keep sketchbook-journals based on their reactions to the reading. For Writing Assignment 3, students will write a letter to **persuade** Jerry to sell the chocolates.

The **nonfiction reading assignment** is tied in with Writing Assignment 1 and the introductory lesson. Students are required to read a piece of nonfiction related in some way to *The Chocolate War*. In this case, the topics are assigned in Lesson One. After reading their nonfiction pieces, students will fill out a worksheet on which they answer questions regarding facts, interpretation, criticism, and personal opinions. During one class period, students make **oral presentations** about the nonfiction pieces they have read. This not only exposes all students to a wealth of information, it also gives students the opportunity to practice **public speaking**.

The **review lesson** pulls together all of the aspects of the unit. The teacher is given four or five choices of activities or games to use which all serve the same basic function of reviewing all of the information presented in the unit.

The **unit test** comes in two formats: all multiple choice-matching-true/false or with a mixture of matching, short answer, and composition. As a convenience, two different tests for
each format have been included.

There are additional **support materials** included with this unit. The **extra activities packet** includes suggestions for an in-class library, crossword and word search puzzles related to the novel, and extra vocabulary worksheets. There is a list of **bulletin board ideas** which gives the teacher suggestions for bulletin boards to go along with this unit. In addition, there is a list of **extra class activities** the teacher could choose from to enhance the unit or as a substitution for an exercise the teacher might feel is inappropriate for his/her class. **Answer keys** are located directly after the **reproducible student materials** throughout the unit.

UNIT OBJECTIVES *The Chocolate War*

1. Through reading *The Chocolate War* students will analyze characters and their situations to better understand the themes of the novel.

2. Students will demonstrate their understanding of the text on four levels: factual, interpretive, critical, and personal.

3. Students will practice reading aloud and silently to improve their skills in each area.

4. Students will enrich their vocabularies and improve their understanding of the novel through the vocabulary lessons prepared for use in conjunction with it.

5. Students will answer questions to demonstrate their knowledge and understanding of the main events and characters in *The Chocolate War*.

6. Students will practice writing through a variety of writing assignments.

7. The writing assignments in this are geared to several purposes:
    a. To check the students' reading comprehension
    b. To make students think about the ideas presented by the novel
    c. To make students put those ideas into perspective
    d. To encourage critical and logical thinking
    e. To provide the opportunity to practice good grammar and improve students' use of the English language.

READING ASSIGNMENT SHEET - *Anne Frank*

Date Assigned	Chapters	Completion Date
	1-5	
	6-13	
	14-19	
	20-26	
	27-32	
	33-39	

Date Assigned	Writing Assignment	Completion Date
	1	
	2	
	3	
	Nonfiction Assignment	
	Project	

UNIT OUTLINE - *Chocolate War*

1	2	3	4	5
Writing Assignment #1	Library/Research	Writing Conference Research	Non-Fiction Presentations	PVR 1-5
6 Study ?s 1-5 Writing Assignment 2	**7** PVR 6-13 Mini-Lesson Foreshadowing	**8** Study ?s 3-13 Mini-Lesson Character Traits	**9** PVR 14-19	**10** Study ?s 14-19 Mini-Lesson Conflict
11 PVR 20-26 Oral Reading Evaluation	**12** Study ?s 20-26 Mini Lesson Mood	**13** PVR 27-32	**14** Study ?s 27-32 Mini Lesson Figurative Lang.	**15** PVR 33-39
16 Study ?s 33-39 Finish Earlier Assignments	**17** Extra Discussion ?s	**18** Writing Assignment 3	**19** Group Projects	**20** Presentation of Projects
21 Vocabulary Review	**22** Unit Review	**23** Unit Test		

Key: P = Preview Study Questions   V = Prereading Vocabulary Worksheet   R = Read   RA = Reading Assignment

STUDY QUESTIONS

SHORT ANSWER STUDY QUESTIONS *The Chocolate War*

Chapters 1-5
1. What does Jerry discover about himself during football practice?
2. Who is Obie and how does he feel about Archie?
3. Why is Obie especially disgruntled this day?
4. What is an "Assignment"?
5. What does Archie notice about Renault while watching football practice?
6. What does Obie regret as he watches the football practice?
7. What do the shadows of the goal posts resemble?
8. Describe the bus stop confrontation Jerry has with the hippie.
9. Why does Brother Leon call Archie into his room after school?
10. What task does Archie assign Goober to do for the Vigils?
11. Explain what the black box is.

Chapters 6-13
1. Summarize the incident in class between Brother Leon and Bailey.
2. How does the author describe Emile Janza?
3. Was Goober successful in completing his assignment in Room 19? If so, what helped him complete the task? If not, why not?
4. Describe the relationship between Jerry and his father.
5. What was Archie's opinion of the way Brother Leon conducted the chocolate sale?
6. Archie told The Vigils that Brother Leon's need for support from them was symbolic. Of what was it symbolic?
7. Describe the scene in Room 19. Include Brother Leon's reaction and Archie's response.
8. Did the incident in Room 19 occur before or after the chocolate sale started?
9. Did Jerry get his Assignment before or after Goober finished his?
10. What was Jerry's response when Brother Leon asked him if he would sell the chocolates?

Chapters 14-19
1. Who was the treasurer for the chocolate sale, and how did he get the job?
2. What was the irony about Archie's picture of Emile?
3. Summarize the meeting between Brother Leon and David Caroni.
4. On the day after Jerry's Assignment ended, Brother Leon called the roll for the chocolate sale. What did Jerry say when Brother Leon called his name.
5. Jerry learned where the secret of Brother Leon lurked. Where was it?
6. What did Jerry realize about the Assignment?
7. Did Jerry figure out why he had said no to selling the chocolates?
8. What did the kid on the bus say to Jerry?
9. What were the words on the poster in Jerry's locker?

Chocolate War Study Questions Page 2

10. How did Jerry feel after he said no this time? (end of chapter 19)

Chapters 20-26
1. Describe the ritual in Brother Jacques's class. Include how it was ended.
2. How did Obie feel about the Assignments and his relationship with Archie?
3. Summarize the conversation between Archie and Obie when they met in the gym.
4. What was happening to the sales? (Chapter 22)
5. What was Brother Leon's explanation for the way the sales were?
6. What did Goober tell Jerry he was going to do? Why?
7. What information did Cochran overhear Brothers Jacques and Leon discussing?
8. Summarize the phone conversation between Archie and Leon.
9. What was Jerry's new Assignment? What would happen if he didn't carry it out?
10. What new feeling did Jerry have?

Chapters 27-32
1. Describe Frankie Rollo. Summarize what happened when The Vigils summoned him to a meeting.
2. According to Carter, what problem did The Vigils have?
3. What solution did Archie propose? What did he say about Jerry?
4. Describe the things that happened to Jerry. (Chapter 28)
5. How was the chocolate being sold?
6. What did Goober discover when he watched Cochran post the latest results? How did he react?
7. Summarize the confrontation between Janza and Jerry.

Chapters 33-39
1. What happened to Jerry at school after the beating? (Chapter 34)
2. What was Archie's plan to get rid of Jerry's chocolates?
3. What did Archie tell Jerry about the fight?
4. What was the twist to the raffle tickets?
5. What color marble did Archie choose?
6. What went wrong with the fight?
7. Who was watching the fight from the top of the hill? Who saw him there?
8. Who confronted Archie? What did he say? Who came to Archie's rescue?
9. What happened to Jerry at the end of the story?
10. What happened to the chocolates and the money from the raffle?

ANSWER KEY: STUDY QUESTIONS *The Chocolate War*

Chapters 1-5

1. What does Jerry discover about himself during football practice?
   He realizes he has guts.

2. Who is Obie and how does he feel about Archie?
   He is the secretary for The Vigils. He openly criticizes Archie, but is drawn to his power and charm.

3. Why is Obie especially disgruntled this day?
   He fears he may lose his job if he continues to be late.

4. What is an "Assignment"?
   It is something (like a prank) Archie thinks up for someone to do to be in the secret membership of The Vigils. He specializes in psychological exercises rather than violent measures.

5. What does Archie notice about Renault while watching football practice?
   He observes his toughness and stubbornness when he refuses to give up out on the field after being wiped out.

6. What does Obie regret as he watches the football practice?
   He regrets not going out for football and instead being involved in something he can't even tell his parents.

7. What do the shadows of the goal posts resemble?
   They resemble a network of crosses, empty crucifixes.

8. Describe the bus stop confrontation Jerry has with the hippie.
   The guy accuses Jerry of staring at them every day, which he does. He also calls him "square boy" and tells him he's missing a lot of things in the world because he's caught up in his mundane routine.

9. Why does Brother Leon call Archie into his room after school?
   Leon is desperate to make sure the candy sells and wants to enlist the help of The Vigils.

10. What task does Archie assign Goober to do for The Vigils?
    He is to loosen every screw that holds anything together in Brother Eugene's room on Thursday night.

11. Explain what the black box is.

    The black box was a tradition of The Vigils to attempt some control over assignments. It contains six marbles; five of them white and one of them black. If the Assigner drew a white marble, the assignment went as ordered. If he drew the black marble, the Assigner had to perform the assignment. Archie had beaten the black box for three years.

Chapters 6-13

1. Summarize the incident in class between Brother Leon and Bailey.

    Brother Leon accused Bailey of cheating, and slapped him on the cheek. Bailey insisted he had not cheated. The rest of the class was silent during this dialog, until one of the boys anonymously called out to let Bailey alone. Leon held the class after the bell rang, and told them they had turned the classroom into Nazi Germany. He said Bailey was the only brave one in the room, because he remained true to himself.

2. How does the author describe Emile Janza?

    He describes Emile as a brute, although he did not look like one. He was small and not too strong, even though he was a tackle on the football team. He realized that no one wanted trouble, and he used this knowledge to harass teachers and students.

3. Was Goober successful in completing his assignment in Room 19? If so, what helped him complete the task? If not, why not?

    Yes, he was successful. After he had been there for six hours, a group of masked boys came in and helped him. They finished the task in another three hours.

4. Describe the relationship between Jerry and his father.

    They had a routine of work and school. They did not talk much, and never shared feelings.

5. What was Archie's opinion of the way Brother Leon conducted the chocolate sale?

    He thought Brother Leon had dramatized it too much and put everyone on the spot.

6. Archie told The Vigils that Brother Leon's need for support from them was symbolic. Of what was it symbolic?

    It was a symbol of the power The Vigils had at the school.

7. Describe the scene in Room 19. Include Brother Eugene's reaction and Archie's response.

    The author compared it to someone dropping The Bomb. It took 37 seconds for all of the furniture to collapse. Brother Eugene stood at his desk and cried. Archie was watching from the hallway when Brother Leon grabbed him and angrily dug his fingernails into Archie's shoulder while accusing him of making it happen. Archie denied it. He was angry that Brother Leon had spoiled his moment of triumph.

8. Did the incident in Room 19 occur before or after the chocolate sale started?
   It happened before the sale started.

9. Did Jerry get his Assignment before or after Goober finished his?
   Jerry got his Assignment after Goober had completed his.

10. What was Jerry's response when Brother Leon asked him if he would sell the chocolates?
    He said, "No."

Chapters 14-19

1. Who was the treasurer for the chocolate sale, and how did he get the job?
   Brian Cochran was the treasurer. Brother Leon had "volunteered" him.

2. What was the irony about Archie's picture of Emile?
   There was no picture.

3. Summarize the meeting between Brother Leon and David Caroni.
   Caroni had received an *F* on a test. This was surprising because he was an *A* student. In a discussion with Brother Leon, Caroni realized that Leon was blackmailing him with the test grade. Leon suggested that he might change the grade if Caroni told him why Renault was not selling the chocolate. Caroni told Leon about the Assignment. Leon said he might reconsider the test grade at the end of the semester. Caroni left the meeting thinking that life was rotten.

4. On the day after Jerry's Assignment ended, Brother Leon called the roll for the chocolate sale. What did Jerry say when Brother Leon called his name.
   He said that he would not sell the chocolates.

5. Jerry learned where the secret of Brother Leon lurked. Where was it?
   It was in his eyes.

6. What did Jerry realize about the Assignment?
   It was cruel, and cruelty sickened him.

7. Did Jerry figure out why he had said no to selling the chocolates?
   No, he did not.

8. What did the kid on the bus say to Jerry?
   He said that Jerry had guts; he wished he had thought of saying no to selling things.

9. What were the words on the poster in Jerry's locker?
    The poster's words were: *Do I dare disturb the universe?*

10. How did Jerry feel after he said no this time? (end of Chapter 19)
    He felt a deep and penetrating sadness.

Chapters 20-26
1. Describe the ritual in Brother Jacques's class. Include how it was ended.
    Every time Brother Jacques said the word "environment" the class members would stand up. This had been going on for a week. One day when Brother Jacques had used the word "environment" six times in fifteen minutes, Obie realized that Archie had told Brother Jacques about the prank, and now Brother Jacques had turned the tables on the boys.

2. How did Obie feel about the Assignments and his relationship with Archie?
    He was tired of the Assignments. He hated Archie, and was tired of picking up after him.

3. Summarize the conversation between Archie and Obie when they met in the gym.
    Obie told Archie that by still refusing to sell the chocolates, Jerry was defying The Vigils. Archie replied that no one could defy them and get away with it.

4. What was happening to the sales? (Chapter 22)
    They were going down.

5. What was Brother Leon's explanation for the way the sales were?
    He said the boys had been infected by apathy. He blamed Jerry.

6. What did Goober tell Jerry he was going to do? Why?
    He said he was going to quit the football team. He said there was evil in the school. He didn't like what The Vigils did to the boys or to the teachers.

7. What information did Cochran overhear Brothers Jacques and Leon discussing?
    Jacques said Leon was abusing his power of attorney, and had over-extended the school's finances.

8. Summarize the phone conversation between Archie and Leon.
    Leon blamed Archie and The Vigils for the poor sales. He told Archie that if the sale was a failure, The Vigils would go down the drain.

9. What was Jerry's new Assignment? What would happen if he didn't carry it out?
    His new Assignment was to sell the chocolates. Archie told him the punishment would be worse than the assignment.

10. What new feeling did Jerry have?
    He felt like bridges were burning behind him. He didn't care about it.

Chapters 27-32
1. Describe Frankie Rollo. Summarize what happened when The Vigils summoned him to a meeting.
    Rollo was a troublemaker, not easily intimidated. He did not participate in activities, and he did not do homework. He made a comment to Archie and The Vigils about their ineffectiveness at getting Jerry to sell the chocolates. Carter hit Rollo, then had him carried out.

2. According to Carter, what problem did The Vigils have?
    The problem was that they had become involved with the chocolate sale, and then let Jerry make fools of them.

3. What solution did Archie propose? What did he say about Jerry"
    Archie said they should make the sale popular and get it over quickly. He said Jerry would end up wishing he had sold the chocolates.

4. Describe the things that happened to Jerry. (Chapter 28)
    He was hit from behind in the kidneys during football practice. Twice that night he answered the phone and only heard a chuckle. The next day he found that the poster in his locker had been smeared with paint, and his sneakers had been slashed. Another day he went to art class and discovered that his watercolor was missing.

5. How was the chocolate being sold?
    Teams of boys were gong out and selling it. Credit was distributed among the boys, so that it looked like more and more of them were meeting their quotas.

6. What did Goober discover when he watched Cochran post the latest results? How did he react?
    He watched Cochran record a number fifty next to his(Goober's) name. He knew this was false, because he stopped selling at twenty-seven boxes in support of Jerry. He didn't feel anything when he saw it,, but he started crying.

7. Summarize the confrontation between Janza and Jerry.
    Jerry had been dismissed early from football practice. Janza confronted him, and accused Jerry of being queer. Then four or five other boys came out from behind the bushes and beat Jerry up.

Chapters 33-39

1. What happened to Jerry at school after the beating? (Chapter 34)
    He became invisible to the students and teachers.

2. What was Archie's plan to get rid of Jerry's chocolates?
    He was going to raffle them off.

3. What did Archie tell Jerry about the fight?
    He said it would be a way to get even. The fight would be with Janza, and would be under control.

4. What was the twist to the raffle tickets?
    Each boy who bought a ticket could decide on a punch, and who should deliver it.

5. What color marble did Archie choose?
    He got one of the white marbles.

6. What went wrong with the fight?
    The Vigils had not warned the boys that no illegal punches would be allowed. When Carter called the first illegal punch, he realized it was too late to stop it. The fight got out of control.

7. Who was watching the fight from the top of the hill? Who saw him there?
    Obie saw Brother Leon watching from the top of the hill.

8. Who confronted Archie? What did he say? Who came to Archie's rescue?
    Brother Jacques confronted Archie, and said they had barely averted a riot. He wanted to know why Archie had organized the fight. Leon entered then, and said he realized Archie had done everything for the school.

9. What happened to Jerry at the end of the story?
    He was taken away in an ambulance.

10. What happened to the chocolates and the money from the raffle?
    The boys raided the chocolates. The money was safe with Cochran.

MULTIPLE CHOICE STUDY/QUIZ QUESTIONS *The Chocolate War*

<u>Chapters 1-5</u>

1. During football practice Jerry discovers
    - A. he can't get the death of his mother out of his mind.
    - B. he has guts.
    - C. pains in places he never knew existed.
    - D. there are fellows watching him by the seats in the stadium.

2. Obie is
    - A. the secretary to The Vigils and Archie's stooge.
    - B. fired from his job for being late one last time.
    - C. overjoyed at the attention Archie gives him.
    - D. the Assigner for The Vigils.

3. Obie is especially mad at Archie this day because
    - A. he is missing football practice.
    - B. he is tired of Archie's assignments injuring innocent people.
    - C. he may lose his job for being late again.
    - D. he can't tell his parents about the Vigils.

4. True or False: An Assignment was given to every freshman entering Trinity.
    - A. True
    - B. False

5. During football practice Archie notices Renault's
    - A. bloody nose.
    - B. submission to the coach.
    - C. toughness and stubbornness.
    - D. lack of coordination.

6. True or False: Obie regrets being involved in The Vigils.
    - A. True
    - B. False

7. The goal posts resemble
    - A. clotheslines.
    - B. scarecrows.
    - C. crucifixes.
    - D. windmills.

8. True or False: Brother Leon is the Chairman of the Board at Trinity.
    A. True
    B. False

9. Archie assigns Goober to
    A. sell all his chocolates for him.
    B. sabotage Brother Leon's room.
    C. unscrew the chairs and desks in Brother Jacques's room.
    D. take the gas out of ten cars in the parking lot.

10. The black box contains
    A. twelve blue marbles and one yellow cat's eye marble.
    B. red and white marbles.
    C. one black and some white marbles.
    D. equal number of green and orange marbles.

Chapters 6-11

1. True or False: Brother Leon accused Bailey of lying.
    A. True
    B. False

2. Brother Leon told the boys they had turned the classroom into
    A. Dante's Inferno.
    B. the Inquisition.
    C. Nazi Germany.
    D. Orwell's 1984.

3. True or False: Emile Janza was a brute who liked to harass teachers and students.
    A. True
    B. False

4. True or False: Jerry and his father had a very close relationship. They talked a lot.
    A. True
    B. False

5. What was Archie's opinion of the way Brother Leon conducted the chocolate sale?
    A. He liked the way Brother Leon was handling it.
    B. He thought Brother Leon was too easy on the kids.
    C. He thought they should have to sell more chocolates.
    D. He thought Brother Leon had dramatized it too much.

6. True or False: Archie said that Brother Leon's need for support from The Vigils was symbolic of the power The Vigils had at the school.
    A. True
    B. False

7. Which of these did **not** happen in Room 19?
    A. The author compared it to someone dropping The Bomb.
    B. It took 37 seconds for all of the furniture to collapse.
    C. Brother Eugene was crushed when the bookcase fell on top of him.
    D. Archie watched from the hallway.

8. Did the incident in Room 19 occur before or after the chocolate sale started?
    A. It happened before the sale started.
    B. It happened after the sale started.

9. Did Jerry get his Assignment before or after Goober finished his?
    A. Jerry got his Assignment before Goober had completed his.
    B. Jerry got his Assignment after Goober had completed his.

10. What was Jerry's response when Brother Leon asked him if he would sell the chocolates"
    A. He said, "Yes."
    B. He said, "No."

Chapters 14-19

1. True or False: Brian Cochran got the treasurer's job because he wanted to be an accountant.
    A. True
    B. False

2. What was the irony about Archie's picture of Emile?
    A. Archie had already destroyed the picture.
    B. It was a picture of someone else.
    C. Archie had already posted it on the bulletin board.
    D. There had never been a picture.

3. Whom was Leon trying to blackmail?
    A. Mario Delamo
    B. Tubs Casper
    C. David Caroni
    D. Paul Consalvo

4. On the day after Jerry's Assignment ended, Brother Leon called the roll for the chocolate sale. What did Jerry say when Brother Leon called his name?
    A. He said that he would not sell the chocolates.
    B. He said he would sell the chocolates.

5. Jerry learned where the secret of Brother Leon lurked. Where was it?
    A. It was locked away in a safe deposit box.
    B. It was in his eyes.
    C. It was in his prayer book.
    D. It was in his handshake.

6. True or False: Jerry realized the Assignment was cruel.
    A. True
    B. False

7. Did Jerry figure out why he had said no to selling the chocolates?
    A. Yes, he did.
    B. No, he did not.

8. What did the kid on the bus say to Jerry?
    A. He said Jerry had no school spirit.
    B. He threatened to boycott the pharmacy where Jerry's father worked.
    C. Nothing. The kid ignored Jerry.
    D. He said that Jerry had guts; he wished he had thought of saying no.

9. What were the words on the poster in Jerry's locker?
    A. *Do not go harshly into that good night.*
    B. *He marches to the tune of a different drummer*
    C. *Do I dare disturb the universe?*
    D. *To thine own self be true.*

10. How did Jerry feel after he said "no" this time? (end of Chapter 19)
    A. He felt a deep and penetrating sadness.
    B. He felt great.
    C. He felt like a weight had been lifted.
    D. He felt angry and defiant.

Chapters 20-26

1. How did Brother Jacques find out about the prank with the word "environment"?
    A. He figured it out for himself.
    B. Jerry told him.
    C. Archie told him.
    D. Brother Eugene told him.

2. True or False: Obie hated Archie, and was tired of picking up after him.
    A. True
    B. False

3. Who told Archie that Jerry was defying The Vigils by refusing to sell the chocolates?
    A. Brother Leon
    B. Goober
    C. Brother Eugene
    D. Obie

4. What was happening to the sales? (Chapter 22)
    A. They were going down.
    B. They were going up.

5. What was Brother Leon's explanation for the way the sales were?
    A. He said The Vigils were not helping enough.
    B. He said the parents were not supportive.
    C. He said the boys had been infected by Jerry's apathy.
    D. He said the boys did not understand the importance of the sale.

6. What did Goober say was wrong with the school?
    A. Too many non-Catholics went to the school
    B. He said the Brothers were too greedy.
    C. He said there was evil in the school.
    D. He said the football team was not good enough.

7. What information did Cochran overhear Brothers Jacques and Leon discussing?
    A. Jacques said the Headmaster was going to die soon.
    B. Leon said the candy only cost him fifty cents a box, and they would make a lot of money.
    C. They wre planning to take the money and run away with it.
    D. Jacques said Leon was abusing his power of attorney, and had over-extended the school's finances.

8. Who told Archie that if the sale was a failure, The Vigils would go down the drain?
    A. Jerry
    B. Brother Leon
    C. Carter
    D. Obie

9. What was Jerry's new Assignment?
    A. He was to apologize to Brother Leon.
    B. He was to sell the chocolates.
    C. He was to eat all 50 boxes of chocolates in one day.
    D. He was to transfer out of the school immediately.

10. True or False: Jerry felt like bridges were burning behind him. He didn't care about it.
    A. True
    B. False

Chapters 27-32

1. Who made the comment about the ineffectiveness of The Vigils?
    A. Frankie Rollo
    B. Carlson
    C. John Sulkey
    D. Mike Terasigni

2. Who said The Vigils' problem was that they had become involved with the chocolate sale, and then let Jerry make fools of them?
    A. Brother Leon
    B. Jerry
    C. Carter
    D. Obie

3. True or False: Carter said they should make the sale popular and get it over quickly.
    A. True
    B. False

4. Which of the following did **not** happen to Jerry? (Chapter 28)
    A. He was hit from behind in the kidneys during football practice.
    B. The poster in his locker had been smeared with paint
    C. His new sneakers had been replaced with a pair of pink girl's sneakers.
    D. His watercolor for art class was missing.

5. True or False: Each boy was meeting his own quota.
    A. True
    B. False

6. Who had stopped selling at twenty-seven boxes in support of Jerry?
    A. the boy on the bus
    B. Bailey
    C. Darcy
    D. Goober

7. Of what did Janza accuse Jerry?
    A. Janza accused Jerry of being a heretic.
    B. Janza accused Jerry of being a snob.
    C. Janza accused Jerry of taking steroids to improve his football performance.
    D. Janza accused Jerry of being queer.

Chapters 33-39

1. What happened to Jerry at school after the beating? (Chapter 34)
    A. He became belligerent.
    B. He stayed home for a week.
    C. He became invisible to the students and teachers.
    D. A lot of the boys felt sorry for him.

2. What was Archie's plan to get rid of Jerry's chocolates?
    A. He was going to hold Jerry for ransom until his father paid for the chocolates.
    B. He was going to pay for them himself, then lie and say Jerry had sold them.
    C. He was going to force Cochran to alter the books.
    D. He was going to hold a raffle.

3. True or False: Goober thought the fight would be a good way for Jerry to get even.
    A. True
    B. False

4. True or False: Each boy who bought a ticket could hit Jerry.
    A. True
    B. False

5. What color marble did Archie choose?
    A. He got the black one.
    B. He got one of the white marbles.

6. What went wrong with the fight?
    A. Janza refused to play by the rules.
    B. Jerry was wearing brass knuckles.
    C. The Vigils had not warned the boys that no illegal punches would be allowed.
    D. Someone from the stands shot Jerry.

7. Who was watching the fight from the top of the hill? Who saw him there?
    A. Brother Jacques was watching. Jerry saw him.
    B. Archie saw Mr. Renault watching.
    C. Carter saw the Headmaster watching.
    D. Obie saw Brother Leon watching from the top of the hill.

8. Who confronted Archie?
    A. Brother Jacques
    B. Mr. Renault
    C. Goober
    D. Brother Leon

9. What happened to Jerry at the end of the story?
    A. He was taken away in an ambulance.
    B. He died in the stadium.
    C. He walked away, triumphant.
    D. Goober drove him home.

10. What happened to the chocolates and the money from the raffle?
    A. The boys ate the chocolates. Archie kept the money.
    B. Archie kept the chocolates and gave the money to Brother Leon.
    C. The boys raided the chocolates. The money was safe with Cochran.
    D. No one knew what happened to either the money or the chocolates.

STUDENT ANSWER SHEET-MULTIPLE CHOICE/QUIZ QUESTIONS

Chapters 1-5	Chapters 6-13	Chapters 14-19
1.	1.	1.
2.	2.	2.
3.	3.	3.
4.	4.	4.
5.	5.	5.
6.	6.	6.
7.	7.	7.
8.	8.	8.
9.	9.	9.
10.	10.	10.

Chapters 20-26	Chapters 27-32	Chapters 33-39
1.	1.	1.
2.	2.	2.
3.	3.	3.
4.	4.	4.
5.	5.	5.
6.	6.	6.
7.	7.	7.
8.	8.	8.
9.	9.	9.
10.	10.	10.

ANSWER KEY-MULTIPLE CHOICE/QUIZ QUESTIONS

	Chapters 1-5		Chapters 6-13		Chapters 14-19
1.	B	1.	B False	1.	B False
2.	A	2.	C	2.	D
3.	C	3.	A True	3.	C
4.	B False	4.	B False	4.	A
5.	C	5.	D	5.	B
6.	A True	6.	A True	6.	A True
7.	C	7.	C	7.	B
8.	B False	8.	A	8.	D
9.	C	9.	B	9.	C
10.	C	10.	B	10.	A

	Chapters 20-26		Chapters 27-32		Chapters 33-39
1.	C	1.	A	1.	C
2.	A True	2.	C	2.	D
3.	D	3.	B False	3.	B False
4.	A	4.	C	4.	B False
5.	C	5.	B False	5.	B
6.	C	6.	D	6.	C
7.	D	7.	D	7.	D
8.	B			8.	A
9.	B			9.	A
10.	A True			10.	C

PREREADING VOCABULARY WORKSHEETS

VOCABULARY WORKSHEET *The Chocolate War*

Chapters 1-5

Part I: Using Prior Knowledge and Context Clues
Below are the sentences in which the vocabulary words appear in the text. Read the sentence. Use any clues you can find in the sentence combined with your prior knowledge, and write what you think the underlined words mean on the lines provided.

1. But when he tried to get up, his body ***mutinied*** against movement.
   _____

2. He was unwilling to abandon this lovely ***lassitude***, but he had to, of course.
   _____

3. Archie turned and smiled at him ***benevolently***, like a goddam king handing out favors.
   _____

4. He moved with a subtle rhythm, ***languidly***, the walk of an athlete, although he hated all sports and had nothing but contempt for athletes.
   _____

5. Obie smiled in delicious ***malice***.
   _____

6. The shadows of the goal posts definitely resembled a network of crosses, empty ***crucifixes***.
   _____

7. He studied the magazine ***surreptitiously*** and then closed the magazine and put it back where it belonged, on the top shelf.
   _____

8. Finally, tired of smuggling it into the bathroom for swift ***perusals***, and weary of his deceit, and haunted by the fear that his mother would find the magazine, Jerry had sneaked it out of the house and dropped it into a catchbasin.
   _____

9. On the surface, he was one of those pale, ***ingratiating*** kind of men who tiptoed through life on small, quick feet.
   _____

10. His thin, high voice ***venomous***.
   _____

11. Archie was surprised by Leon's ***audacity,*** knowing his connection with The Vigils and bringing him in here this way.
   _____

12. "Thursday," Archie said with a command in his voice, no nonsense, final, ***irrevocable***.
   _____

13. The black box was his ***nemesis***.
   _____

Part II: Determining the Meaning   Match the vocabulary words to their dictionary definitions.

1.	mutinied	A.	in a kind manner; with good will
2.	lassitude	B.	boldness
3.	benevolently	C.	faintness
4.	languidly	D.	with indifference
5.	malice	E.	readings
6.	crucifixes	F.	spite; ill-will
7.	surreptitiously	G.	wheedling
8.	perusals	H.	underhandedly
9.	ingratiating	I.	poisonous
10.	venomous	J.	crosses with the figure of Christ crucified
11.	audacity	K.	revolted
12.	irrevocable	L.	downfall; antagonist
13.	nemesis	M.	irreversible

Chocolate War Vocabulary
Chapters 6-13
Part I: Using Prior Knowledge and Context Clues
Below are the sentences in which the vocabulary words appear in the text. Read the sentence. Use any clues you can find in the sentence combined with your prior knowledge, and write what you think the underlined words mean on the lines provided.

1. As if the class and Leon were banded together in a secret ***conspiracy***.

2. Leon's voice softened, "I know you wouldn't consider anything so ***sacrilegious***. "

3. Watching her ebb away, seeing her beauty diminish, witnessing the awful ***alteration*** of her face and body was too much for Jerry to bear.

4. And, without warning, the ***anguish*** of her loss returned, like a blow to his stomach, and he was afraid that he would faint.

5. Through some nightmarish miracle, he was able to ***superimpose*** the image of his mother's face on his father's - and for a moment the echo of all her sweetness was there and he had to go through all the horror of visualizing her in the coffin again.

6. That pathetic holdup try by a scared young kid ***brandishing*** a toy pistol?

7. Archie had to admit that the Brother turned in one of his great performances. Academy Award ***caliber.***

8. He poured it on like Niagara- school spirit, the traditional sale that never failed, the need for funds to keep this magnificent ***edifice*** of education operating on all gears.

9. Witnessing the ***pandemonium***, he knew that this was one of his major triumphs.

10. He watched Leon storing away, pushing his way through the *__tumultuous__* corridor, disappearing into the swarming stream of boys.

_____

Part II: Determining the Meaning   Match the vocabulary words to their dictionary definitions.

1. conspiracy
2. sacrilegious
3. alteration
4. anguish
5. superimpose
6. brandishing
7. caliber
8. edifice
9. pandemonium
10. tumultuous

A. change
B. to lay on something else
C. quality
D. structure
E. irreverent; profane
F. chaos, disorder
G. waving
H. plot
I. agony; grief
J. riotous, noisy

Chocolate War Vocabulary
Chapters 14-19
Part I: Using Prior Knowledge and Context Clues
Below are the sentences in which the vocabulary words appear in the text. Read the sentence. Use any clues you can find in the sentence combined with your prior knowledge, and write what you think the underlined words mean on the lines provided.

1. He had expected Carter to blitz and instead the big guard had pulled back and skirted the line, ***annihilating*** Jerry from behind.
   _____

2. "Good, good, good, good." The coach's voice, ***raucous*** in triumph.
   _____

3. Despite the ***adulation*** of the guys at school, he felt as if there was some kind of distance between him and the fellows.
   _____

4. He remembered with a glow when he went up to the stage for his award last year and how the Headmaster had talked about Service To The School, and how "John Sulkey ***exemplified*** these special attributes."
   _____

5. He remembered with a glow when he went up to the stage for his award last year and how the Headmaster had talked about Service To The School, and how "John Sulkey exemplified these special ***attributes***."
   _____

6. He also had to do it ***furtively***, afraid that his father or mother might see him.
   _____

7. Brian shrugged, tabulating his own totals once more to be sure that Brother Leon wouldn't blame him for any ***discrepancies***.
   _____

8. Were teachers as ***corrupt*** as the villains you read about in books or saw in movies and television?
   _____

9. All of this in his mind, of course, as he tossed in his bed, the sheet twisted around him like a ***shroud***, suffocating him.
   _____

10. Aware of his ***mortality***, he turned over again, entangled in his bedclothes.
    _____

11. He was a nut, known for his lack of ***inhibitions***, his complete disregard of the rules.
    _____

Part II: Determining the Meaning Match the vocabulary words to their dictionary definitions.

1. annihilating   A. praise; worship
2. raucous   B. qualities
3. adulation   C. destroying
4. exemplified   D. differences; contradictions
5. attributes   E. wicked; dishonest
6. furtively   F. cloak, grave clothes
7. discrepancies   G. loud, harsh
8. corrupt   H. humanity
9. shroud   I. fears, misgivings
10. mortality   J. secretly
11. inhibitions   K. represented, illustrated

Chocolate War Vocabulary
Chapters 20-26

Part I: Using Prior Knowledge and Context Clues
Below are the sentences in which the vocabulary words appear in the text. Read the sentence. Use any clues you can find in the sentence combined with your prior knowledge, and write what you think the underlined words mean on the lines provided.

1. And he evidently didn't know what to do about it and so he didn't do anything, figuring apparently that the thing would run its course and why risk a *futile* showdown when it was obviously a prank.
   _____

2. "I think maybe the Renault kid's got the right idea, after all," Kevin said, his mouth thick with peanut butter which gave his words more *resonance*, like a disc jockey's.
   _____

3. Brian shrugged and continued, calling out the names in singsong fashion, with measured pauses, letting his voice linger over the names and numbers, a weird *litany* there in the quiet office.
   _____

4. Infected by a disease we could call *apathy*.
   _____

5. He had never spoken to Leon on the telephone before and the *disembodied* voice at the other end of the line had caught him off balance.
   _____

6. The *malingerers*, the malcontents,-they always rally around a rebel. Renault must sell the chocolates.
   _____

7. The malingerers, the *malcontents*,-they always rally around a rebel. Renault must sell the chocolates.
   _____

8. For the first time, the word brought *exultancy* to him, a lifting of the spirit.
   _____

43

9. He was still ***buoyant*** when he arrived home, otherwise, he wouldn't have had the courage to actually call the girl.
   _____

10. Wasn't refusing to sell the chocolates a kind of ***perversion***?
    _____

Part II: Determining the Meaning   Match the vocabulary words to their dictionary definitions.

1. futile
2. resonance
3. litany
4. apathy
5. disembodied
6. malingerers
7. malcontents
8. exultancy
9. buoyant
10. perversion

A. grumblers, complainers
B. prayer
C. slackers, shirkers
D. joy; jubilation
E. indifference
F. ringing; resounding
G. divested; stripped
H. useless
I. enthusiastic
J. deviation, abnormality

Chocolate War Vocabulary
Chapters 27-32

Part I: Using Prior Knowledge and Context Clues
Below are the sentences in which the vocabulary words appear in the text. Read the sentence. Use any clues you can find in the sentence combined with your prior knowledge, and write what you think the underlined words mean on the lines provided.

1. A junior, Rollo was ***insolent***, a troublemaker.

2. He stood loose and easy, ***unintimidated.***

3. Rollo didn't respond but the smirk on his face was an ***eloquent*** answer.

4. Carter paused to let them imagine the ***dissolution*** of The Vigils.

5. "How come *we're* wrong?" Obie, the ***perennial*** straight man, called out.

6. Suddenly, he was struck from behind, a ***vicious*** blow to his kidneys, sickening in its impact.

7. The chuckle turned into a hoot of ***derision***.

8. The school was ***notorious*** for "borrowers"- kids who weren't exactly thieves but walked off with anything that wasn't nailed down or locked up.

9. His poster had been smeared with ink, or some kind of blue paint. The message had been virtually ***obliterated***.

10. He was ***fastidious*** and ordinarily taught math but had been filling in for the regular art teacher.

11. "Well, Renault, perhaps I *do* make a habit of losing landscapes, after all," he said, and Jerry felt a rush of ***camaraderie*** for the teacher.

    _____

12. Only five thousand to go-or four thousand, nine hundred and ninety to be exact, as Brother Leon pointed out in that fussy ***meticulous*** way of his.

    _____

Part II: Determining the Meaning Match the vocabulary words to their dictionary definitions.

1. insolent   A. articulate; well-spoken
2. unintimidated   B. cruel; brutal
3. eloquent   C. companionship; friendship
4. dissolution   D. ridicule; mockery
5. perennial   E. painstaking; precise
6. vicious   F. demolished
7. derision   G. persnickety; particular
8. notorious   H. sassy; disrespectful
9. obliterated   I. enduring; lasting
10. fastidious   J. well-known
11. camaraderie   K. fearless; bold
12. meticulous   L. breaking up

Chocolate War Vocabulary
Chapters 33-39

Part I: Using Prior Knowledge and Context Clues
Below are the sentences in which the vocabulary words appear in the text. Read the sentence. Use any clues you can find in the sentence combined with your prior knowledge, and write what you think the underlined words mean on the lines provided.

1. More ***paranoia***, he chided himself, trudging along the path that led from the football field to the gym.

2. The laughter surprised Jerry- he'd expected ***retaliation***.

3. One misstep would send him hurtling into the depths below ***oblivion***.

4. A ***parody*** of those long ago childhood pleadings.

5. The ***desecrated*** poster had been removed and the wall scrubbed clean.

6. Leon's ***rancid*** breath- didn't he ever eat anything else but bacon, for crissakes- filled the air as he stood beside Brian looking over the tabulations.

7. Ah, the hell with it, Brian thought as Leon's voice droned on ***sanctimoniously.***

8. Obie smiled ***maliciously*** when he caught Archie standing there in surprise.

9. The pain in his neck was ***excruciating***- his head had snapped back from the impact of Janza's fist.

10. He had never struck someone like that before, in fury, premeditated, and he'd enjoyed ***catapulting*** all his power toward the target, the release of all his frustrations, hitting back at last, lashing out, getting revenge finally, revenge not only against Janza but all that he represented.

   _____

11. There was ***rebuke*** in his voice but a gentle, guarded rebuke, not the hostility he had revealed to Archie

   _____

Part II: Determining the Meaning Match the vocabulary words to their dictionary definitions.

   1. paranoia   A. revenge
   2. retaliation   B. self-righteously
   3. oblivion   C. rank; offensive
   4. parody   D. spitefully
   5. desecrated   E. blackness; nothingness
   6. rancid   F. extremely painful
   7. sanctimoniously   G. distrust; suspicion
   8. maliciously   H. hurling; flinging
   9. excruciating   I. imitation; take-off
   10. catapulting   J. scolding
   11. rebuke   K. defiled; violated

ANSWER KEY: VOCABULARY WORKSHEETS *The Chocolate War*

Chapters 1-5	Chapters 6-13	Chapters 14-19
1. K	1. H	1. C
2. C	2. E	2. G
3. A	3. A	3. A
4. D	4. I	4. K
5. F	5. B	5. B
6. J	6. G	6. J
7. H	7. C	7. D
8. E	8. D	8. E
9. G	9. F	9. F
10. I	10. J	10. H
11. B		11. I
12. M		
13. L		

Chapters 20-26	Chapters 27-32	Chapters 33-39
1. H	1. H	1. G
2. F	2. K	2. A
3. B	3. A	3. E
4. E	4. L	4. I
5. G	5. I	5. K
6. C	6. B	6. C
7. A	7. D	7. B
8. D	8. J	8. D
9. I	9. F	9. F
10. J	10. G	10. H
	11. C	11. J
	12. E	

DAILY LESSONS

LESSON ONE

Objectives
1. To develop research skills
2. To write to inform by developing and organizing facts to convey information
3. To complete Writing Assignment #1 and the Nonfiction Assignment

Activity

Assign one of the following topics (or topics of your choice) to each of the students. Distribute Writing Assignment #1 and the Nonfiction Assignment sheet and discuss them. Students should fill out the Nonfiction Assignment sheet for at least one of the sources they used and submit it along with their report. Take students to the library for the rest of the period to work on the assignment.

Topics
1. Gangs, secret societies, or fraternities/sororities in the general society.

2. Gangs, secret societies, or fraternities/sororities in schools.

3. The use of fund raisers in schools.

4. The use of fund raisers in the general public.

5. Different types of funding for public and private schools.

6. Differences/similarities between public and private schools.

7. Peer pressure.

8. Abuse of power by an authority figure.

9. Blackmail.

10. Advertising campaigns.

11. Private schools in a local area, or across the country.

12. Interview someone who works for a fund raising organization and find out how such sales are conducted.

WRITING ASSIGNMENT #1 *The Chocolate War*
Writing to Inform

PROMPT
You are reading a fictional account of some events that took place in the life of one teen-aged boy, Jerry Renault. In this story, he encounters a great deal of peer pressure in the form of a secret society at his high school. In order to develop your understanding of the themes in the novel, you will be asked to do some research before you begin reading.

PREWRITING
Your teacher may assign a topic or allow you to choose one. You will then go to the library to research the topic. Look for encyclopedias, books, magazine articles, videos, newspapers, and Internet sources. You may want to interview an expert on the topic of your choice.

Think of questions you have about your topic. Write each one on a separate index card. Then read to find the answers, and write them on the cards. Also take notes on interesting and important facts, even if you did not have questions about them. Put each fact on a separate card. Make sure to cite your references. That means to write down the title of the book or article, the author, and the page number for each one.

Arrange your note cards in the order you want to use for your paper. Number them, perhaps in the upper right hand corner. Read through them to make sure they make sense in that order. Rearrange as necessary.

DRAFTING
Introduce your topic in the first paragraph. Tell why you chose it, and give a preview of what the rest of the paper will be about. Then write several paragraphs about the topic. Each paragraph should have a main idea and supporting details. Your last paragraph should summarize the information in the report.

PEER CONFERENCE/REVISING
When you finish the rough draft, ask another student to look at it. You may want to give the student your note cards so he/she can double check for you and see that you have included all of the information. After reading, he or she should tell you what he/she liked best about your report, which parts were difficult to understand or needed more information, and ways in which your work could be improved. Reread your report considering your critic's comments and make the corrections you think are necessary.

PROOFREADING/EDITING
Do a final proofreading of your report, double-checking your grammar, spelling, organization, and the clarity of your ideas.

WRITING EVALUATION FORM *The Chocolate War*

Name _____ Date _____ Class _____

Writing Assignment # _____

Circle One For Each Item:

Composition	excellent	good	fair	poor
Style	excellent	good	fair	poor
Grammar	excellent	good	fair	poor (errors noted)
Spelling	excellent	good	fair	poor (errors noted)
Punctuation	excellent	good	fair	poor (errors noted)
Legibility	excellent	good	fair	poor (errors noted)

Strengths:

Weaknesses:

Comments/Suggestions:

NONFICTION ASSIGNMENT SHEET *The Chocolate War*
(To be completed after reading the required nonfiction article)

Name _____ Date _____ Class/ _____

Title of Nonfiction Read _____

Author _____ Publication Date _____

I. **Factual Summary:** Write a short summary of the piece you read.

II. **Vocabulary:**
    1. Which vocabulary words were difficult?

    2. What did you do to help yourself understand the words?

III. **Interpretation:** What was the main point the author wanted you to get from reading his/her work?

IV. **Criticism:**
    1. Which points of the piece did you agree with or find easy to believe? Why?

    2. With which points of the piece did you disagree or find difficult to believe? Why?

V. **Personal Response:**
    1. What do you think about this piece?

    2. How does this piece help you better understand the novel *The Chocolate War*?

LESSON TWO

Objectives
    1. To continue doing library research for the nonfiction assignment
    2. To write to inform

Activity #1
    Either take the students to the library or give them time in class to work on their research projects.

Activity #2
    While the writing conferences are scheduled for Lesson Three, you may want to begin them during Lesson Two if some of the students are ready. Establish a quiet section of the room for the conferences.

LESSON THREE

Objectives
    1. To participate in a writing conference with the teacher
    2. To revise the nonfiction assignment based on the suggestions made during the writing conference

Activity #1
    Choose a quiet location in the room to hold the writing conferences.

Activity #2
    Students should be working independently on their research projects when they are not conferencing.

LESSON FOUR

<u>Objectives</u>
1. To widen the breadth of students' knowledge about the topics discussed or touched upon in *The Chocolate War*
2. To check students' non-fiction assignments

<u>Activity</u>

Ask each student to give a brief oral report about the nonfiction work he/she read for the nonfiction assignment. Your criteria for evaluating this report will vary depending on the level of your students. You may wish for students to give a complete report without using notes of any kind, or you may want students to read directly from a written report, or you may want to do something in between these two extremes. Just make students aware of your criteria in ample time for them to prepare their reports.

Start with one student's report. After that, ask if anyone else in the class has read on a topic related to the first student's report. If no one has, choose another student at random. After each report, be sure to ask if anyone has a report related to the one just completed. That will help keep a continuity during the discussion of the reports.

LESSON FIVE

Objectives
1. To preview *The Chocolate War* Unit
2. To receive books and other related materials (study guides, reading assignment)
3. To relate prior knowledge to the new material
4. To become familiar with the vocabulary for Chapters 1-5
5. To preview the study questions for Chapters 1-5
6. To read Chapters 1-5

Activity #1
Distribute the <u>Chocolate Quiz</u> and give students time to work on it. Discuss the answers with the class.

Activity #2
Ask students to describe any fund-raising activities in which they have participated. Then tell students they are going to read a story about a school that has a chocolate sale, and what happens to one boy during the sale.

Activity #3
Distribute the materials students will use in this unit. Explain in detail how students are to use these materials.

<u>Study Guides</u> Students should preview the study guide questions before each reading assignment to get a feeling for what events and ideas are important in that section. After reading the section, students will (as a class or individually) answer the questions to review the important events and ideas from that section of the book. Students should keep the study guides as study materials for the unit test.

<u>Reading and Writing Assignment Sheet</u> Either post a completed assignment sheet on a side blackboard or bulletin board and leave it there for students to see each day, or duplicate copies for each student to have. In either case, you should advise students to become very familiar with the reading assignments so they know what is expected of them.

<u>Unit Outline</u> You may find it helpful to distribute copies of the Unit Outline to your students so they can keep track of upcoming lessons and assignments. You may also want to post a copy of the Unit Outline on a bulletin board and cross off each lesson as you complete it.

Extra Activities Center The resource sections of this unit contain suggestions for a library of related books and articles in your classroom as well as crossword and word search puzzles. Make an extra activities center in your room where you will keep these materials for students to use. Bring the books and articles in from the library and keep several copies of the puzzles on hand. Explain to students that these materials are available for students to use when they finish reading assignments or other class work early.

Books Each school has its own rules and regulations regarding student use of school books. Advise students of the procedures that are normal for your school.

Notebook or Unit Folder You may want the students to keep all of their worksheets, notes, and other papers for the unit together in a binder or notebook. During the first class meeting, tell them how you want them to arrange the folder. Make divider pages for vocabulary worksheets, prereading study guide questions, review activities, notes, and tests. You may want to give a grade for accuracy in keeping the folder.

Activity #4

Do a group KWL Sheet with the students (form included.) Students should know something about fund-raising activities and peer pressure after completing the research projects, and will have information to share. Put this information in the K column (What I Know.) Ask students what they want to find out from reading *The Chocolate War* and record this in the W column (What I Want to Find Out.) Keep the sheet and refer back to it after reading the book. Complete the L column (What I Learned) at that time.

Activity #5

Work through the prereading vocabulary worksheet for Chapters 1-5 with the students. Tell them they will have a sheet like this to complete before reading each section of the book.

Activity #6

Show students how to preview the study questions for Chapters 1-5. Encourage students to predict what they think answers might be, to write down their predictions, and to compare these with their answers after reading the chapters.

Activity #6

Begin reading Chapter 1 aloud to the class. Invite willing students to continue reading aloud until the end of the class period. Tell students to complete the reading before the next class meeting.

LESSON SIX

Objectives
1. To review the main ideas and themes in Chapters 1-5
2. To begin Writing Assignment #2

Activity #1

Discuss the answers to the Study Guide questions for Section 1 in detail. Write the answers on the board or overhead projector so students can have the correct answers for study purposes. Encourage students to take notes. If the students own their books, encourage them to use high lighter pens to mark important passages and the answers to the study guide questions.

Note: It is a good practice in public speaking and leadership skills for individual students to take charge of leading the discussion of the study questions. Perhaps a different student could go to the front of the class and lead the discussion each day that the study questions are discussed during this unit. Of course, the teacher should guide the discussion when appropriate and be sure to fill in any gaps the students leave.

Activity #2 (Writing Assignment #2)

Tell students they will be keeping a sketchbook-journal as Writing Assignment #2. Explain that a sketchbook-journal is a combination of sketches about and written responses to the story. They will be required to make an entry for each chapter in the novel.

Students can sketch memorable scenes from the chapters, or paste in magazine pictures that remind them of the events in the chapter.

The written entries should focus on each student's response to the literature, and should not merely be a plot summary. They should include comments about their thoughts and feelings while reading, any questions they have, and predictions for the next chapter. For *The Chocolate War*, encourage them to write about the mood of the story, as well as the plot and character development.

It is up to the individual teacher to decide how to grade or respond to the journals, and whether to have students share them with the class or keep them private.

THE CHOCOLATE QUIZ

Write the name of the chocolate candy bar under the definition.

Alexander Dumas and his heroes would like this candy bar.	Another name for the galaxy
The home of the movie stars	Author of *The Gift of the Magi*
A famous street in New York City	It was not named for a famous baseball player, but for the daughter of a president.
Two words describing a feline	Two feminine gender pronouns
An affectionate touching with the lips	Superman's news reporter alias
The fourth planet from the sun, also called the red planet.	Partly stifled laughs

ANSWER KEY: THE CHOCOLATE QUIZ

THREE MUSKETEERS	MILKY WAY
HOLLYWOOD	O. HENRY
FIFTH AVENUE	BABY RUTH
KIT KAT	HER SHE Y
KISS	CLARK
MARS	SNICKERS

KWL *The Chocolate War*

Directions: Before reading, think about what you already know about Robert Cormier and/or *The Chocolate War*. Write the information in the K column. Think about what you would like to find out from reading the book. Write your questions in the W column. After you have read the book, use the L column to write the answers to your questions from the W column, and anything else you remember from the book.

K **What I Know**	**W** **What I Want to Find Out**	**L** **What I Learned**

WRITING ASSIGNMENT #2 *The Chocolate War*
Journal Writing to Express a Personal Opinion

PROMPT

For this unit, you will be asked to keep a sketchbook- journal. This is a combination of sketches about and written responses to a story. You will be required to make an entry for each chapter in the novel.

First, decide on the format for your sketchbook-journal. Spend some time decorating your cover and setting up the book. Make sure to include the title of each chapter and the page numbers in you copy of the book. Also date each entry.

You can sketch memorable scenes from the chapters, paste in magazine pictures , or use computer clip art.. Even if you do not consider yourself a good artist, try to make some sketches. Use colors that remind you of the mood of the story. You may want to take photographs and put them in the sketchbook-journal.

The written entries should focus on your response to the literature, and should not merely be chapter summaries. They should include comments about your thoughts and feelings while reading, any questions you have, and predictions about the next chapter. Try to write at least one page for each entry. You, your class mates and your teacher will decide whether to share the journals or keep them private.

Here are some suggestions for the types of entries you may want to make.

Check Your Understanding	Explain how the story is making sense to you. Give examples and note page numbers. Establish the setting, mood, point of view, and character relationships. Discuss the stated themes.
Make Inferences	Explain your thoughts about the feelings and motives of the characters. Discuss the implied themes.
Make and Revise Predictions	At the end of each chapter, make a prediction about what you think will happen next. After you read, go back and check your predictions. Tell if you had to revise them, and why.
Ask Questions	Ask questions about scenes or events that are confusing. Record the answers if you discuss the questions in class, or later find the answer in the novel.
Give Your Opinion	Give your opinion about the literary quality of the work. Discuss the author's style, use of language, and use of literary devices. Tell why you do nor do not like the story. Tell how you feel while reading the chapters. Compare the book with others you have read.

Make Connections   Think about ways the characters and events relate to your own life and experiences. Put yourself in the character's place and discuss how you would think or feel in that situation. Try this from the point of view of the main character and a few of the minor ones.

Make Recommendations   Tell what you think the characters should do or say. Tell how you would end the story, or what you think might happen next.

LESSON SEVEN

Objectives
    1. To become familiar with the vocabulary for Chapters 6-13
    2. To preview the study questions for Chapters 6-13
    3. To identify examples of foreshadowing
    3. To read Chapters 6-13
    4. To predict Jerry's Assignment

Activity #1

    Write the vocabulary words on the board. Ask students if any of the words are familiar. Encourage students to guess the meanings of the words. Then distribute copies of the prereading vocabulary worksheet. Let students work in pairs or small groups to complete the page. Check answers.

Activity #2

    Have volunteers read the study questions aloud to the class. Encourage students to predict the answers.

Activity #3 Minilesson: Foreshadowing

    In foreshadowing, the author gives clues or hints about future developments or occurrences. Read the first sentence aloud to students, or write it on the board. Discuss how it could be a foreshadowing of events yet to come in the novel. Then have them look at Chapter 2, where it says, "It made Obie uncomfortable to think of that stuff", and discuss the foreshadowing.

    Encourage students to keep a list of events and comments that are examples of foreshadowing. Tell them they will discuss these again during Lesson Seventeen.

Activity #4

    Have small groups of students read one of the chapters from 6 through 12 and give a brief report or skit based on the chapter. Hold the presentations in sequential order.

Activity #5

    Ask students to predict what Jerry's Assignment might be. Then read Chapter 13 with them. Discuss their predictions and the clues they used in the chapter to discover Jerry's Assignment. Remind students to complete the study questions before the next class period.

LESSON EIGHT

Objectives
1. To discuss the main ideas and events in Chapters 6-13
2. To analyze main characters by developing character sketches

Activity #1
Give each student four 1"x2" strips of colored paper or index cards--one blue, one yellow, one green, one pink. Have them put a large letter A on the blue paper, B on the yellow, C on the green, and D on the pink. Distribute copies of the Multiple Choice/Quiz questions for Chapters 12-15. Ask students to read the first question and hold up the colored paper for the correct answer. Then have them mark the correct answer on their worksheets.

Activity #2 Minilesson: Character Development
Explain that an author creates characters by giving them traits such as physical attributes, thoughts, and feelings. The author develops these traits by telling what the characters say, do, and think. Writers usually base their characters at least in part on a real person or persons, and then elaborate. A good writer will make the characters believable for the readers.

Explain that this is a "coming-of-age" story, where the central character becomes more aware of himself because of events that occur. In this novel, the awareness comes because of Jerry's experience during the chocolate sale.

Have students begin by looking for Jerry's character traits as they begin reading. Help them begin filling in the Character Trait Chart (included.) Tell them they should continue to be aware of Jerry's character as they read, and that they will continue the discussion and complete more of the chart during Lesson Seventeen.

Although Jerry is the main character, Archie, Brother Leon, and Goober are also somewhat developed. You may want to assign students to also do character sketches for one of these characters.

LESSON NINE

Objectives
1. To become familiar with the vocabulary words for Chapters 14-19
2. To preview the study questions for Chapters 14-19
3. To read Chapters 14-19

Activity #1

Give students about ten minutes to complete the prereading vocabulary worksheet. Then play a variation on the game of "Hangman", called "The Chocolate Box." Draw an empty box on the board. Next to it, draw spaces for the letters in one of the vocabulary words. Invite students to guess the letters in the word. If a student guesses incorrectly, you draw a circle in the box, putting in a piece of chocolate. Play either until students have guessed the word, or filled the box with chocolates.

Activity #2

Read the questions for Chapter 14 aloud. Then have students read the text silently until they find the answer. Continue in this manner until all questions have been asked and chapters have been read.

CHARACTER TRAITS CHART *The Chocolate War*

CHARACTER _____

CHARACTER TRAIT _____ EVENTS THAT SHOW THAT TRAIT:	**CHARACTER TRAIT** _____ EVENTS THAT SHOW THAT TRAIT:
CHARACTER TRAIT _____ EVENTS THAT SHOW THAT TRAIT:	**CHARACTER TRAIT** _____ EVENTS THAT SHOW THAT TRAIT:

LESSON TEN

Objectives
    1. To discuss the main events and ideas in Chapters 14 -19
    2. To identify the conflicts in the novel

Activity #1
    Divide students into small groups. Have each group prepare the answer to one question, and present the answer to the class.

Activity #2 Minilesson: Conflict
    Tell students that conflict is one of the most important aspects of a work of fiction. The conflict usually is an obstacle to the main character's goal. It usually brings about some type of change in the main character. You may want to use examples from stories the students have previously read, or examples from literature for younger children to illustrate the various types of conflict. Dorothy in *The Wizard of Oz* has a conflict with nature because the tornado takes her away from her home. The conflict between Cinderella and her wicked step-mother is an example of character vs. character. In *The Little Engine That Could*, the little engine is not sure of its ability to take the train over the mountain, illustrating the character vs. himself conflict. The Greek myth of Atalanta illustrates character vs. character as well as character vs. society. Atalanta was expected to marry the man her father chose, but she did not wish to do so. This created the conflict between the two characters. Also, it was traditional for the father to choose the daughter's spouse, and Atalanta rebelled against this tradition. Have students begin filling out the Conflict Chart after they have read the assignment. Discuss their findings. Encourage them to look for more examples of conflict as they read.

LESSON ELEVEN

Objectives
    1. To become familiar with the vocabulary for Chapters 20-26
    2. To preview the study questions for Chapters 20-26
    3. To read Chapters 20-26

Activity #1
    Divide students into groups of ten. Give each group one of the vocabulary words to learn. Have each group teach their word to the class. Then have students complete the vocabulary worksheet.

Activity #2
    Keep the same groups as for the vocabulary work. Assign a question to each group and have the group prepare the answer.

Activity #3
    Depending on the needs of your students, either read the chapters aloud or silently. Remind students that any reading not done in class should be completed by the next class period.

ORAL READING EVALUATION *The Chocolate War*

Name_____   Class_____ Date _____

SKILL	EXCELLENT	GOOD	AVERAGE	FAIR	POOR
FLUENCY	5	4	3	2	1
CLARITY	5	4	3	2	1
AUDIBILITY	5	4	3	2	1
PRONUNCIATION	5	4	3	2	1
_____	5	4	3	2	1
_____	5	4	3	2	1

TOTAL _____ **GRADE** _____

COMMENTS:

CONFLICT CHART *The Chocolate War*

Directions: Use the chart below to record examples of the different types of conflicts you read about.

TYPE OF CONFLICT	STORY	EXAMPLE OF CONFLICT
CHARACTER VS. NATURE		
CHARACTER VS. SELF		
CHARACTER VS. SOCIETY		
CHARACTER VS. CHARACTER		

LESSON TWELVE

Objectives

    1. To discuss the main ideas and events in Chapters 20-26
    2. To discuss the mood and tone of the novel

Activity #1

    Have each group discuss the answer to their assigned question. Remind students to take notes on all of the answers.

Activity #2 Minilesson: Mood

    The mood or tone of a story is the author's attempt to create the atmosphere of story. The mood evokes an emotional response from the reader and lets the reader know how the characters feel. It may stay the same throughout a story, or it may change, depending on circumstances and events. The author's descriptions and the characters' dialogue and actions express the mood of the story. Mood can be stated or implied.

    Ask the students to give their impressions of the mood conveyed by the title and jacket artwork. Have them reread the first chapter of the book to see where and how the mood changes from relatively pleasant to fearful. Make a list of words that Cormier uses to invoke a certain mood. You may want to keep this as a chart or bulletin board that students can add to throughout the unit. Tell students to keep the mood of the book in mind as they read. They will have the opportunity to discuss mood again during Lesson Seventeen.

LESSON THIRTEEN

Objectives

    1. To become familiar with the vocabulary for Chapters 27-32
    2. To preview the study guide questions for Chapters 27-32
    3. To read Chapters 27-32

Activity #1

    Give students about ten or fifteen minutes to complete the prereading vocabulary worksheet and look over the study guide questions.

Activity #2

    Let students choose whether to read the chapters alone silently, or read aloud quietly with a partner. Remind them to complete the reading and answer the study guide questions before the next class meeting.

LESSON FOURTEEN

Objectives
    1. To discuss the main ideas and events in Chapters 27-32
    2. To identify figurative language in the novel

Activity #1
    Invite students to give their answers to the study guide questions.

Activity #2 Minilesson: Figurative Language
    Figures of speech are literary devices that give the writer a non-literal way to describe images and events. Use the following chart to give examples of the different figures of speech. Then write "like a lens focusing" on the board. (Cormier uses this description of Jerry's vision on the first page of The *Chocolate War.*) Ask students to identify the type of figure of speech (simile.) Talk about the literal meaning. Distribute the Figure of Speech worksheet and have students work in small groups to find examples in the novel. If you want the students to continue recording examples in the remaining chapters, assign a due date for the worksheet.

FIGURES OF SPEECH

Figures of speech are literary devices that give the writer a non-literal way to describe images and events. The main types of figures of speech are hyperbole, irony, metaphor, metonymy, onomatopoeia, paradox, personification, and simile.

<u>CLICHÉ</u>	A cliché is an expression that has been used repeatedly, and has lost its appeal. For example: *white as snow, bright and early.*
<u>HYPERBOLE</u>	Extreme exaggeration used to describe a person or thing. For example: *She had as many pairs of shoes as there are stars in the sky.*
<u>IRONY</u>	The use of words to express something different from and often opposite to their literal meaning. *Sitting in school on a lovely spring day is my favorite thing to do.*
<u>METAPHOR</u>	A comparison without the words like or as. For example, *The cat is a bag of bones.*
<u>METONYMY</u>	A figure of speech in which one word or phrase is substituted for another with which it is closely associated, as in the use of *Washington* for the United States government or of *the sword* for military power.
<u>ONOMATOPOEIA</u>	The use of words such as *buzz* or *splash* that imitate the sounds associated with the objects or actions they refer to.
<u>PARADOX</u>	A seemingly self-contradictory statement that has some truth to it.
<u>PERSONIFICATION</u>	Attributing human characteristics to inanimate objects, animals, or ideas, as in *the wind howled.*
<u>SIMILE</u>	A comparison using the words like or as.

FIGURES OF SPEECH

Figures of speech are literary devices that give the writer a non-literal way to describe images and events. The main types of figures of speech are hyperbole, irony, metaphor, metonymy, onomatopoeia, paradox, personification, and simile. Use the following chart to record examples of figures of speech used in *The Chocolate War*. A sample has been done for you. Note: You may not find an example of each figure of speech in the novel.

Figure of Speech	**Example from Novel, page #**	**Literal Meaning**
simile	like a lens focusing p. 7	Jerry's vision was getting clearer.

LESSON FIFTEEN

Objectives
1. To become familiar with the vocabulary for Chapters 33-39
2. To preview the study questions for Chapters 33-39
3. To read Chapters 33-39

Activity #1

Have students work in pairs to complete the vocabulary worksheet and go over the study guide questions.

Activity #2

Depending on the needs of your students, either have them read the chapters alone silently, or take turns reading them aloud. Remind them that any reading not done in class must be completed before the next class period. Answers to the comprehension questions will also be due at that time.

LESSON SIXTEEN

Objectives
1. To discuss the main ideas and events in Chapters 33-39
2. To complete any unfinished worksheets

Activity #1

Arrange students in small groups and have them discuss the answers to the study guide questions. Circulate among the groups and offer assistance as necessary.

Activity #2

Give students the rest of the class time to complete any minilesson worksheets, or to catch up on vocabulary or study questions they may have missed.

LESSON SEVENTEEN

Objective
    To discuss *The Chocolate War* at the interpretive and critical levels

Activity #1
    Choose the questions from the Extra Writing Assignments/Discussion Questions which seem most appropriate for your students. A class discussion of these questions is most effective if students have been given the opportunity to formulate answers to the questions prior to the discussion. To this end, you may either have all the students formulate answers to all the questions, divide the class into groups and assign one or more questions to each group, or you could assign one question to each student in your class. The option you choose will make a difference in the amount of class time needed for this activity.

Activity #2
    After students have had ample time to formulate answers to the questions, begin your class discussion of the questions and the ideas presented by the questions. Be sure students take notes during the discussion so they have information to study for the unit test.

EXTRA WRITING ASSIGNMENT/DISCUSSION QUESTIONS *The Chocolate War*

<u>Interpretation</u>

1. From what point of view is the story written? How does this affect our understanding of the story?

2. What are the main conflicts in the story? Are they resolved? If so, how? If not, why not?

3. What is the setting? How important is the setting to the story? Why?

4. What does the hippie in Chapter 1 represent?

5. Write a character sketch of one of the following: Jerry, Archie, Brother Leon, Goober.

6. Why was the Assignment so disturbing to Jerry?

7. Why did Archie act the way he did?

8. Is there a significance to Archie's name? The Vigils' name? If so, what is it?

9. In Chapter 4, how do you think Archie felt when he said the words "The Vigils" out loud to Brother Leon for the first time? How does this change the balance of power in the school?

10. Which seemed to be most difficult for Jerry to deal with?

11. Why do you think Brother Leon reacted the way he did when Jerry refused to sell the chocolates?

12. What was the greatest danger/obstacle that Jerry faced? Why do you think so?

13. How long was Goober in Room 19?

14. In Chapter 9, why did Jerry ask his father if things were really okay at the store?

15. In Chapter 9, Jerry remembered watching his father act the part of a doctor one day. Did Mr. Renault have some disappointment about not being a doctor?

16. Why did Jerry think of Gregory Bailey at the end of Chapter 9?

17. What were Brother Leon's motives in increasing the amount of chocolates the boys were to sell?

18. Why did Archie crave chocolate? Is this significant?

19. In Chapter 28, why did Brother Andrew say he would take another look for Jerry's landscape?

20. How are the goalposts symbolic of a crucifix?

Critical

21. Is the story believable? Why or why not?

22. How did Jerry change over the course of the novel? Were these changes for the better?

23. Did any of the other characters change? Which ones, and how?

24. Were the characters believable? Why or why not?

25. The author often used vivid language to describe a scene or event. Give an example of his use of vivid language that you found most effective. Tell why it was effective.

26. What was the overall mood of the story? Give examples to support your answer.

27. Identify a few of the examples of personification and discuss their contribution to the novel.

28. How does the author create suspense?

29. What is the role/importance of the black box? The black marble?

30. What problem or conflict does the author use to get the story started? How effective is it?

31. Could any of the main events be left out? Which ones? Why or why not?

32. Could you change the order of the main events and still have the same outcome? If not, how would the outcome change if the order of the events were changed?

33. How would the story have to change to have a different ending?

34. How would the story change if there were a different narrator?

35. Were you able to predict the ending? What clues did the author give?

36. Discuss the author's use of language. Is it natural? Do people you know talk the way the characters did?

37. Does the mood of the story change? How does the author show this?

38. What words does the author use to create the atmosphere of the book?

39. Which chapter was most important? Why?

40. Were the descriptions in the book effective? Give some examples.

41. Which senses did the descriptions cause you to use? Give examples of the descriptions using hearing, seeing, touching, smelling, taste.

42. Compare and contrast one of the characters in this book with a character in another book.

43. Discuss your reaction to the way Brother Leon presented his lesson on Nazi Germany in Chapter 6.

Personal Response
44. Did you enjoy reading *The Chocolate War?* Why or why not?

45. Is *The Chocolate War* a good title for the book? Why or why not? If not, what title would you suggest?

46. Do you think the Brothers will dissolve The Vigils? Why or why not?

47. If you were the headmaster at Trinity, what would you do about The Vigils?

48. If you were Jerry or Goober, what would you do about the Assignment?

49. Why didn't the Brothers do anything about The Vigils?

50. You, the reader, did not find out what Jerry's Assignment was until after he had started to carry it out. How did this affect you? Was this an effective plot device?

51. What do you think happened to Jerry at the end of the novel?

52. What do you think Jerry Renault will do next?

53. Do you agree or disagree with Jerry's thought during the fight that he was not disturbing the universe, but he was damaging it?

54. Did you have strong feelings while reading this book? If so, what did the author do to cause those feelings? If not, why not?

55. Will you read more of Robert Cormier's books? Why or why not?

56. Before you read the story, did you think it would be possible for a group of boys to act the way The Vigils did? What do you think after reading the story?

57. Did Jerry's experiences change the way you look at yourself? How?

58. Have you read any other stories similar to *The Chocolate War*? If so, tell about them.

59. Would you recommend this book to another student? Why or why not?

60. What questions would you like to ask Robert Cormier?

61. What was the saddest part? What was the most exciting part?

62. What do you remember most about the story?

63. What picture did the author leave in your mind?

64. What did the book make you think about?

QUOTATIONS *The Chocolate War*

Discuss the significance of the following quotations.

1. "These goddam assignments. Do they think it's easy? And the black box." (Ch 1)

2. "I know that, Archie. But Trinity is special, isn't it? If I didn't think the boys of Trinity could do it, do you think I would take a risk? Aren't we capable of what others aren't?" (Ch. 4)

3. "The Vigils will help." (Ch. 4)

4. "And here's what you do, Goober. You loosen." (Ch. 5)

5. "Bailey, why do you find it necessary to cheat? (Ch. 6)

6. "Aw, let the kid alone." (Ch. 6)

7. "You did well, Bailey. I'm proud of you. You passed the biggest test of all--you were true to yourself."

8. "Fine." (Ch. 9)

9. "My God." (Ch. 11)

10. "You! You did this." "I didn't do anything. I didn't promise anything."(Ch. 11)

11. "No."

12. "Tell you what, Caroni. At the end of the term, when the marks close, I'll review that particular test. Perhaps I'll be fresher then. Perhaps I'll see merit that wasn't apparent before. . . ." (Ch. 16)

13. It's not the Vigils, Goob. They're not in it anymore. It's me." (Ch. 19)

14. "At this period of history, man began to learn more about his environment--" (Ch. 20)

15. "I think maybe that Renault kid's got the right idea, after all." (Ch. 21)

16. "He was supposed to start selling after the Assignment was over. So, now he's defying The Vigils. And a lot of guys know that. We are involved, Archie, whether we want to be or not." (Ch. 21)

84

17. "The boys have become infected, Cochran. Infected by a disease we could call apathy. A terrible disease. Difficult to cure." (Ch. 22)

18. "Look, Jerry. There's something rotten in that school. More than rotten . . . Evil." (Ch. 23)

19. "It's all a game, Goob. Think of it as fun and games. Let them have their fun. Brother Eugene must have been on the borderline, anyway." (Ch. 23)

20. "I'll make it clear to you, Archie. If the sale goes down the drain, you and The Vigils also go down the drain. Believe me . . ." (Ch. 24)

22. "Let me put it this way, Carter. Before the sale is over, Renault will be wishing with all his heart that he had sold the chocolates. And the school will be glad he didn't.'
"You'd better be right, Archie. As far as I'm concerned, you're on probation until the last chocolate's sold." (Ch. 27)

23. "Hello. Who is this?" (Ch. 28)

24. "Your watercolor. The landscape assignment. Today's the final day for handing it in. I don't find yours here."
"I put it on your desk yesterday. I handed it in, Brother."
"Well, Renault, perhaps I do make a habit of losing landscapes, after all. At any rate, let me check further. Perhaps I left it in the teacher's lounge." (Ch. 28)

25. "Know what, Cochran? You're a bright boy. You're cool. You catch on fast." (Ch. 30)

26. "Goober sold his fifty boxes." (Ch. 30)

27. "Because you put on a big act, kid. You try to get by with a sincerity act. But you're not kidding me. You live in the closet."
"What do you mean--closet?"
"That you're hiding in there."
"Hiding what? From whom?"
"From everybody. From yourself, even. Hiding that deep, dark secret."
"What secret?"
"That you're a fairy. A queer. Living in the closet, hiding away." (Ch. 31)

28. "Wanna get even, Renault? Strike back? Get revenge? Show them what you think of their goddam chocolates?" (Ch. 35)

29 "You see, Carter, people are two things: greedy and cruel. So we have a perfect set-up here.

The greed part--a kid pays a buck for a chance to win a hundred. Plus fifty boxes of chocolates. The cruel part--watching two guys hitting each other, maybe hurting each other, while they're safe in the bleachers. That's why it works, Carter, because we're all bastards." (Ch. 36)

30. "Welcome, Archie. I imagine you are the villain here, aren't' you?" (Ch. 37)

31. "It'll be all right, Jerry."
"No, it won't. . .   They tell you to do your thing but they don't mean it. They don't want you to do your thing, not unless it happens to be their think, too. It's a laugh, Goober, a fake. Don't disturb the universe, Goober, no matter what the posters say." (Ch. 38)

32. "You really didn't use your best judgement tonight, Archie. But I realize you did it for the school. For Trinity." (Ch. 38)

33. "Someday, Archie, you'll get yours." (Ch. 39)

LESSON EIGHTEEN

Objective
    To write a persuasive essay

Activity #1
    Engage students in a discussion about school, church, or activity club-related sales. Ask how many have participated in selling something, if they really wanted to, and how they were convinced to participate. Discuss the way in which Jerry was introduced to the chocolate sale, and the methods Brother Leon used to make the boys sell the chocolates. Ask them to think of alternative means of persuading Jerry to sell the chocolates.

Optional Topic
    Feel free to vary the topic for this writing assignment. You may want to let students choose the opposite side of this issue, and write a persuasive essay against having school promotional sales.

Activity #2
    Distribute copies of Writing Assignment #3. Give students the rest of the period to work on the assignment.

Activity #3
    Allow time for students to present thier persuasive essays to the class or to small groups of classmates.

WRITING ASSIGNMENT #3 *The Chocolate War*
Writing to Persuade

PROMPT

Jerry was introduced to the chocolate sale, a traditional activity at Trinity, in a most unusual and negative way. Even after the Assignment time was over, he still refused to sell the chocolates. Pretend to be one of Jerry's classmates, possibly an upper-class student, who is more familiar with the sale. Give Jerry some reasons to participate in the chocolate sale.

PREWRITING

Make a list of the reasons you participate in the chocolate sale, and the reasons why you think Jerry should. Think of statements to support each of your reasons, and list them under each reason. Then number the reasons in order from most to least important.

DRAFTING

Make an introductory statement in which you describe the sale, and state your desire to have Jerry participate. Then use one paragraph for each of your reasons. Use the supporting statements for each reason. Think of arguments Jerry might use against telling the chocolates, and put counter-arguments in your letter. Summarize your request and respectfully ask for a reply from Jerry by a certain date, possibly a week after receiving the letter.

PEER CONFERENCING/REVISING

When you finish the rough draft, ask another student to look at it. You may want to give the student your checklist and notes so he/she can double check for you and see that you have included all of the information. After reading, he or she should tell you what he/she liked best about your persuasive letter, which parts were difficult to understand or needed more information, and ways in which your work could be improved. Reread your persuasive letter considering your critic's comments and make the corrections you think are necessary.

PROOFREADING/EDITING

Do a final proofreading of your persuasive letter, double-checking your grammar, spelling, organization, and the clarity of your ideas.

FINAL DRAFT

Follow your teacher's guidelines for completing the final draft of your paper.

LESSON NINETEEN

Student Objective
 1. To demonstrate understanding of the events and themes in the novel by creating a project.
 2. To work cooperatively in a group

Activity #1
 Allow students to choose one of the following projects. Give them the class period to complete it. If students need more time, you can assign the project as homework or add another day onto the unit plan.

LESSON TWENTY

Student Objectives
 1. To present projects related to The Chocolate War
 2. To be attentive to classmates during presentations

Activity #1
 Invite groups and individuals to share their projects. Encourage students in the audience to ask questions and offer comments.

Activity #2
 Display projects around the room.

PROJECT IDEAS

1. Pick one of the incidents to dramatize. Write dialog for the characters.

2. Design a book cover (front and back and inside flaps).

3. Design a bulletin board (ready to be put up; not just sketched).

4. Design and produce a talk show. Choose one of the story incidents as the topic. The host will interview the various characters. Characters should respond based on thier roles in the book.

5. Work in pairs to create a newspaper or magazine interview with one of the characters. Work together to compose questions for the reporter to ask, and answers from the character. Write up the interview.

6. Write a newspaper article based on one or more of the events in the novel. This will be a factual account, not an interview with a character.

7. Present a booktalk based on the book.

8. The quote on the poster in Jerry's locker, *Dare I Disturb the Universe?* is taken from "The Love Song of J. Alfred Prufrock", by T. S. Eliot. Read the entire poem, and present a reading from it to the class.

9. Write a response to "The Love Song of J. Alfred Prufrock". First, briefly summarize the poem. Then, give a personal opinion.

10. Give a brief autobiographical sketch of Robert Cormier.

11. Make a game based on the novel. Write at least 25 questions and answers for the game. Design a gameboard, playing pieces, and carrying box. Write rules for play.

12. Hold small group discussions related to topics in the book. Assign a recorder and a speaker for each group. The speaker from each group make a report to the class.

13. Present a group debate about a topic from the book Have one group of students take a "pro" side, and the other the "con" side. Possible topics are: Should The Vigils be dissolved? What should happen to Brother Leon? Is it right to expect students to raise funds when they are already paying tuition? Who is responsible for Jerry's injuries? Should Archie be dismissed from The Vigils? Should Archie or any of the other Vigils be dismissed from the school?

14. Design an advertisement for the chocolate sale. This could be a poster to display in a store, a newspaper or magazine ad, or a television or radio commercial.

15. Write a letter from Mr. Renault to the Headmaster, expressing his thoughts and feelings about the events involving Jerry.

16. Write journal entries on the events from the point of view of any one of these characters: Jerry, Goober, Archie, Obie, Carter, Brother Leon.

17. Outline the events that might happen in a sequel.

18. Make an audio or videotape of a portion of the book.

LESSON TWENTY ONE

Student Objective

To review all of the vocabulary work done in this unit

VOCABULARY REVIEW ACTIVITIES

1. Divide your class into two teams and have an old-fashioned spelling or definition bee.

2. Give individuals or groups of students a Vocabulary Word Search Puzzle. The person (group) to find all of the vocabulary words in the puzzle first wins.

3. Give students a Vocabulary Word Search Puzzle without the word list. The person or group to find the most vocabulary words in the puzzle wins.

4. Put a Vocabulary Crossword Puzzle onto a transparency on the overhead projector and do the puzzle together as a class.

5. Give students a Vocabulary Matching Worksheet to do.

6. Use words from the word jumble page to play one of the following games: Put one word at a time on the board and have relay teams race to unscramble it. Distribute letter cards for one word at a time. Have students come to the front of the room and spell out the word.

7. Have students write a story in which they correctly use as many vocabulary words as possible. Have students read their compositions orally. Post the most original compositions on your bulletin board.

8. Have students work in teams and play charades with the vocabulary words.

9. Select a word of the day and encourage students to use it correctly in their writing and speaking vocabulary.

10. Have a contest to see which students can find the most vocabulary words used in other sources. You may want to have a bulletin board available so the students can write down their word, the sentence it was used in, and the source.

11. Assign a word to each student, or let them choose a word. Have them look up the origin of the word, the part of speech, definition, a synonym, and an antonym. Then have them write a sentence using the word. Have students present their information orally to the class, or have them design a word map on paper and display the papers.

LESSON TWENTY TWO

Objective

To review the main ideas presented in *The Chocolate War*

Activity #1

Choose one of the review games/activities included in the packet and spend your class period as outlined there.

Activity #2

Remind students of the date for the Unit Test. Stress the review of the Study Guides and their class notes as a last minute, brush-up review for homework.

REVIEW GAMES / ACTIVITIES

1. Ask the class to make up a unit test for *The Chocolate War*. The test should have 4 sections: multiple choice, true/false, short answer and essay. Students may use 1/2 period to make the test, including a separate answer sheet, then swap papers and use the other 1/2 class period to take a test an open-book test a classmate has devised.

2. Take 1/2 period for students to make up true and false questions (including the answers). Collect the papers and divide the class into two teams. Draw a big tic-tac-toe board on the chalk board. Make one team X and one team O. Ask questions to each side, giving each student one turn. If the question is answered correctly, that student's team's letter (X or O) is placed in the box. If the answer is incorrect, no mark is placed in the box. The object is to get three marks in a row like tic-tac-toe. You may want to keep track of the number of games won for each team.

3. Take 1/2 period for students to make up questions (true/false and short answer). Collect the questions. Divide the class into two teams. You'll alternate asking questions to individual members of teams A & B (like in a spelling bee). The question keeps going from A to B until it is correctly answered, then a new question is asked. A correct answer does not allow the team to get another question. Correct answers are +2 points; incorrect answers are -1 point.

4. Allow students time to quiz each other (in pairs) from their study guides and class notes.

5. Give students a Unit Resource Crossword Puzzle to complete.

6. Divide your class into two teams. Use the Unit Resource crossword words with their letters jumbled as a word list. Student 1 from Team A faces off against Student 1 from Team B. You write the first jumbled word on the board. The first student (1A or 1B) to unscramble the word wins the chance for his/her team to score points. If 1A wins the jumble, go to student 2A and give

him/her a clue. He/she must give you the correct word which matches that clue. If he/she does, Team A scores a point, and you give student 3A a clue for which you expect another correct response. Continue giving Team A clues until some team member makes an incorrect response. An incorrect response sends the game back to the jumbled-word face off, this time with students 2A and 2B. Instead of repeating giving clues to the first few students of each team, continue with the student after the one who gave the last incorrect response on the team.

7. Take on the persona of "The Answer Person." Allow students to ask any question about the book. Answer the questions, or tell students where to look in the book to find the answer.

8. Students may enjoy playing charades with events from the story. Select a student to start. Give him/her a card with a scene or event from the story. Allow the players to use their books to find the scene being described. The first person to guess each charade performs the next one.

9. Play a categories-type quiz game. (A master is included in this Unit Plan). Make an overhead transparency of the categories form. Divide the class into teams of three or four players each. Have each team choose a recorder and a banker. Choose a team to go first. That team will choose a category and point amount. Ask the question to the entire class.(Use the Study Guide Quiz and Vocabulary questions.) Give the teams one minute to discuss the answer and write it down. Walk around the room and check the answers. Each team that answers correctly receives the points. (Incorrect answers are not penalized; they just don't receive any points). Cross out that square on the playing board. Play continues until all squares have been used. The winning team is the one with the most points. You can assign bonus points to any square or squares you choose.

10. Have individual students draw scenes from the book. Display the scenes and have the rest of the class look in their books to find the chapter or section that is being depicted. The first student to find the correct scene then displays his or her picture. When the game is over, collect the pictures and put them in a binder for students to look at during their free time.

NOTE: If students do not need the extra review, omit this lesson and go on to the test.

QUIZ GAME
The Chocolate War

Chapters 1-5	Chapters 6-13	Chapters 14-19	Chapters 20-26	Chapters 27-32	Chapters 33-39
100	100	100	100	100	100
200	200	200	200	200	200
300	300	300	300	300	300
400	400	400	400	400	400
500	500	500	500	500	500

UNIT TESTS

Short Answer Unit Test 1 *The Chocolate War*

I. Matching/Identify

1.	ROLAND GOUBERT	A.	"A" student blackmailed by Leon
2.	ARCHIE	B.	Archie's straight man
3.	BROTHER LEON	C.	New England boy's school
4.	DAVID CARONI	D.	author
5.	EMILE JANZA	E.	was assigned to dismantle a classroom
6.	ROBERT CORMIER	F.	president of The Vigils
7.	TRINITY	G.	turned the prank back on The Vigils
8.	JOHN CARTER	H.	pummeled Jerry
9.	BROTHER JACQUES	I.	temporary Headmaster
10.	OBIE	J.	Vigil assigner

II. Short Answer

1. What is an "Assignment"?

2. Explain what the black box is.

Short Answer Unit Test 1 *The Chocolate War*

3. Summarize the incident in class between Brother Leon and Bailey.

4. What went wrong with the fight?

5. What happened to Jerry at the end of the story?

Short Answer Unit Test 1 *The Chocolate War*

III. Fill-in-the-Blank

The situation at school had been getting more and more difficult for Jerry. One day, after he had been dismissed early from (1) _____ Janza and four or five other boys (2) _____. After that, Jerry became (3) _____ to the students and teachers. He began to enjoy this lack of identity. Later that day, though, someone tried to (4) _____, and he knew he was being noticed again.

By now, all of the chocolates, except for Jerry's 50 boxes, had been sold and accounted for. (5) _____ developed a plan to sell Jerry's chocolates. He held a (6) _____. This was to end in a (7) _____ between Jerry and Janza. Each boy who bought a box of Jerry's chocolates was able to (8) _____ and decide who should deliver it.

At the beginning of the fight, (9) _____ brought out the (10) _____ All four hundred boys watched as Archie pulled out the (11) _____. (12) _____ arrived at the last minute, because he had been reluctant to go to the fight at all. Then something went wrong. The Vigils had not warned the boys about (13) _____, and one was called for. Jerry deflected part of the blow, which angered Janza. Janza began punching Jerry wildly, so when Jerry found an opening, he hit Janza. At that point Jerry realized he was not disturbing the universe, but he was (14) _____. Goober watched and counted as Janza hit Jerry sixteen more times. Then the lights in the field went out. The fight ended as Jerry (15) _____

IV. Essay

Discuss the main themes in the novel. Give examples from the novel.
Use the back of this paper, or another sheet of loose-leaf, to answer the essay question.

Short Answer Unit Test 1 *The Chocolate War*

V. Vocabulary Part 1

Listen to the vocabulary words and spell them. After you have spelled all the words, go back and write down the definitions.

WORD	DEFINITION
1.	
2.	
3.	
4.	
5.	
6.	
7.	
8.	
9.	
10.	

Vocabulary Part 2

Place the letter of the matching definition on the blank line.

1. MUTINIED   A. slackers; shirkers
2. CAMARADERIE   B. underhandedly
3. DERISION   C. extremely painful
4. EXCRUCIATING   D. revolted
5. LANGUIDLY   E. cruel; brutal
6. MALINGERERS   F. with indifference
7. RAUCOUS   G. fearless; bold
8. SURREPTITIOUSLY H. companionship; friendship
9. UNINTIMIDATED   I. loud; harsh
10. VICIOUS   J. ridicule; mocking

Answer Key Unit Test 1 *The Chocolate War*

I. <u>Matching/Identify</u>

E	1.	ROLAND GOUBERT	A.	"A" student blackmailed by Leon
J	2.	ARCHIE	B.	Archie's straight man
I	3.	BROTHER LEON	C.	New England boy's school
A	4.	DAVID CARONI	D.	author
H	5.	EMILE JANZA	E.	was assigned to dismantle a classroom
D	6.	ROBERT CORMIER	F.	president of The Vigils
C	7.	TRINITY	G.	turned the prank back on The Vigils
F	8.	JOHN CARTER	H.	pummeled Jerry
G	9.	BROTHER JACQUES	I.	temporary Headmaster
B	10.	OBIE	J.	Vigil assigner

II. <u>Short Answer</u>

1. What is an "Assignment"?

   It is something (like a prank) Archie thinks up for someone to do to be in the secret membership of The Vigils. He specializes in psychological exercises rather than violent measures.

2. Explain what the black box is.

   The black box was a tradition of The Vigils to attempt some control over assignments. It contains six marbles; five of them white and one of them black. If the Assigner drew a white marble, the assignment went as ordered. If he drew the black marble, the Assigner had to perform the assignment. Archie had beaten the black box for three years.

3. Summarize the incident in class between Brother Leon and Bailey.

   Brother Leon accused Bailey of cheating, and slapped him on the cheek. Bailey insisted he had not cheated. The rest of the class was silent during this dialog, until one of the boys anonymously called out to let Bailey alone. Leon held the class after the bell rang, and told them they had turned the classroom into Nazi Germany. He said Bailey was the only brave one in the room, because he remained true to himself.

4. What went wrong with the fight?

   The Vigils had not warned the boys that no illegal punches would be allowed. When Carter called the first illegal punch, he realized it was too late to stop it. The fight got out of control.

5. What happened to Jerry at the end of the story?
   He was taken away in an ambulance.

III. Fill-in-the -Blank

The situation at school had been getting more and more difficult for Jerry. One day, after he had been dismissed early from (1) ***football practice*** Janza and four or five other boys (2) ***beat him up***. After that, Jerry became (3) ***invisible*** to the students and teachers. He began to enjoy this lack of identity. Later that day, though, someone tried to (4) ***push him down the stairs***, and he knew he was being noticed again.

By now, all of the chocolates, except for Jerry's 50 boxes, had been sold and accounted for. (5) ***Archie*** developed a plan to sell Jerry's chocolates. He held a (6) ***raffle***. This was to end in a (7) ***boxing match*** between Jerry and Janza. Each boy who bought a box of Jerry's chocolates was able to (8) ***call a punch*** and decide who should deliver it.

At the beginning of the fight, (9) ***Obie*** brought out the (10) ***black box*** All four hundred boys watched as Archie pulled out the (11) ***white marble***. (12) ***Goober*** arrived at the last minute, because he had been reluctant to go to the fight at all. Then something went wrong. The Vigils had not warned the boys about (13) ***illegal punches***, and one was called for. Jerry deflected part of the blow, which angered Janza. Janza began punching Jerry wildly, so when Jerry found an opening, he hit Janza. At that point Jerry realized he was not disturbing the universe, but he was (14) ***damaging it***. Goober watched and counted as Janza hit Jerry sixteen more times. Then the lights in the field went out. The fight ended as Jerry (15) ***was taken away by ambulance.***

VI. Essay

Answers will vary, depending on class discussions.

V. Vocabulary Part 1

Listen to the vocabulary word and spell it. After you have spelled all the words, go back and write down the definitions.

Teacher: Choose any of the words from the unit and write them here.

WORD	DEFINITION
1.	
2.	
3.	
4.	
5.	
6.	
7.	
8.	
9.	
10.	

Vocabulary Part 2

Place the letter of the matching definition on the blank line.

D	1.	MUTINIED	A.	slackers; shirkers
H	2.	CAMARADERIE	B.	underhandedly
J	3.	DERISION	C.	extremely painful
C	4.	EXCRUCIATING	D.	revolted
F	5.	LANGUIDLY	E.	cruel; brutal
A	6.	MALINGERERS	F.	with indifference
I	7.	RAUCOUS	G.	fearless; bold
B	8.	SURREPTITIOUSLY	H.	companionship; friendship
G	9.	UNINTIMIDATED	I.	loud; harsh
E	10.	VICIOUS	J.	ridicule; mocking

Short Answer Unit Test 2 *The Chocolate War*

I. <u>Matching/ Identify</u>

1. BEAUTIFUL   A. painted over in Jerry's locker
2. POSTER   B. pummeled Jerry
3. FINE   C. New England boy's school
4. SNEAKERS   D. accused of cheating by Leon
5. TRINITY   E. The Vigils shredded Jerry's
6. UNIVERSE   F. Jerry questioned whether or not to disturb it
7. GREG BAILEY   G. assigned to dismantle a classroom
8. JOHN CARTER   H. Mr. Renault's favorite word
9. ROLAND GOUBERT   I. Archie's expression
10. EMILE JANZA   J. president of The Vigils

1. Who are The Vigils? Who are the key members/officers? What is an "Assignment"?

2. What task does Archie assign Goober to do for The Vigils? Is he successful? Why or why not? Describe what happened as a result of this Assignment.

Short Answer Unit Test 2 *The Chocolate War*

3. Summarize the meeting between Brother Leon and David Caroni.

4. What did Jerry realize about the Assignment?

5. Describe the raffle and the fight. What went wrong with the fight? What happened to Jerry? What happened to Archie?

Short Answer Unit Test 2 *The Chocolate War*

III. Fill-in-the-Blank

     Archie had designed a prank that involved everyone in (1) _____ classroom. Every time the teacher said the word (2) _____, all of the boys had to (3) _____. This had been going on for about a week. One day, when the teacher had used the word six times in fifteen minutes, (4) _____ realized that Archie had (5) _____.

     Obie was (6) _____ the Assignments. He (7) _____ Archie, and was tired of picking up after him. Sometimes Obie regretted not (8) _____, and instead being involved in something he could not discuss with his parents.

     The chocolate sale had not been going well. Brother Leon said the boys had been infected by (9) _____. He blamed (10) _____. He told Archie that if the sale was a failure, (11) _____. Archie then gave Jerry a new Assignment. He was told to (12) _____.

     Jerry did not carry out his new Assignment. One day when he went to his locker, he saw that his poster (13) _____ and his sneakers (14) _____. Another day he went to art class and discovered (15) _____. The punishment was truly turning out to be worse than the Assignment.

IV. Essay

     What are the main conflicts in the novel? Are they resolved? If so, how? If not, why not?

Short Answer Unit Test 2 *The Chocolate War*

V. Vocabulary Part 1
Listen to the vocabulary word and spell it. After you have spelled all the words, go back and write down the definitions.

WORD	DEFINITION
1. _____	_____
2. _____	_____
3. _____	_____
4. _____	_____
5. _____	_____
6. _____	_____
7. _____	_____
8. _____	_____
9. _____	_____
10. _____	_____

Vocabulary Part 2
Place the letter of the matching definition on the blank line.

1. TUMULTUOUS   A. riotous; chaotic
2. SUPERIMPOSE   B. downfall; antagonist
3. RETALIATION   C. difference; abnormality
4. REBUKE   D. revenge
5. PERVERSION   E. faintness
6. PARODY   F. imitation; take-off
7. OBLIVION   G. blackness; nothingness
8. NEMESIS   H. to lay on something else
9. METICULOUS   I. painstaking; precise
10. LASSITUDE   J. scolding

Answer Key Short Answer Unit Test 2 *The Chocolate War*

I. Matching/Identify

Use this key for both Short Answer Unit Test 2 and the Advanced Short Answer Test.

I	1.	BEAUTIFUL	A.	painted over in Jerry's locker
A	2.	POSTER	B.	pummeled Jerry
H	3.	FINE	C.	New England boy's school
E	4.	SNEAKERS	D.	accused of cheating by Leon
C	5.	TRINITY	E.	The Vigils shredded Jerry's
F	6.	UNIVERSE	F.	Jerry questioned whether or not to disturb it
D	7.	GREG BAILEY	G.	assigned to dismantle a classroom
J	8.	JOHN CARTER	H.	Mr. Renault's favorite word
G	9.	ROLAND GOUBERT	I.	Archie's expression
B	10.	EMILE JANZA	J.	president of The Vigils

II. Short Answer

1. Who are The Vigils? Who are the key members/officers? What is an "Assignment"?

    The Vigils are a secret society of boys at Trinity High School. John Carter is the president. Archie thinks up the Assignments and matches each one to a student. Obie keeps everything straight.

    An Assignment is something (like a prank) which Archie thinks up for someone to do to be in the secret membership of the Vigils. He specializes in psychological exercises rather than violent measures.

2. What task does Archie assign Goober to do for The Vigils? Is he successful? Why or why not? Describe what happened as a result of this Assignment.

    He is to loosen every screw that holds anything together in Brother Leon's room on Thursday night. Yes, he was successful. After he had been there for six hours, a group of masked boys came in and helped him. They finished the task in another three hours.

    The author compared the scene in the classroom to someone dropping The Bomb. It took 37 seconds for all of the furniture to collapse. Brother Eugene stood at his desk and cried. Archie was watching from the hallway when Brother Leon grabbed him and angrily dug his fingernails into Archie's shoulder while accusing him of making it happen. Archie denied it. He was angry that Brother Leon had spoiled his moment of triumph.

3. Summarize the meeting between Brother Leon and David Caroni.

    Caroni had received an *F* on a test. This was surprising because he was an *A* student. In a discussion with Brother Leon, Caroni realized that Leon was blackmailing him with the test grade. Leon suggested that he might change the grade if Caroni told him why Renault was not selling the chocolate. Caroni told Leon about the Assignment. Leon said he might reconsider the test grade at the end of the semester. Caroni left the meeting thinking that life was rotten.

4. What did Jerry realize about the Assignment?
It was cruel, and cruelty sickened him.

5. Describe the raffle and the fight. What went wrong with the fight? What happened to Jerry? What happened to Archie?

Archie held a raffle to sell Jerry's chocolates. He arranged for Jerry and Janza to fight each other. Each boy who bought a ticket was allows to call one of the punches.

The Vigils had not warned the boys that no illegal punches would be allowed. When Carter called the first illegal punch, he realized it was too late to stop it. The fight got out of control. Janza and Jerry began punching each other at will, and Janza pummeled Jerry.

Obie saw Brother Leon watching from the top of the hill. Suddenly, the lights went off on the field. The boys started leaving the bleachers, and stole the chocolates. Archie went to the electrical building, where he was confronted by Brother Jacques. He wanted to know why Archie had organized the fight. Leon entered then, and said he realized Archie had done everything for the school.

Goober stayed with Jerry until an ambulance came to take him to the hospital.

III. Fill-in-the-Blank

Archie had designed a prank that involved everyone in (1) ***Brother Eugene's*** classroom. Every time the teacher said the word (2) ***environment*** all of the boys had to (3) ***stand up and move around***. This had been going on for about a week. One day, when the teacher had used the word six times in fifteen minutes, (4) ***Obie*** realized that Archie had (5) ***set them up/told Brother Eugene what was going on***.

Obie was (6) ***tired of*** the Assignments. He (7) ***hated*** Archie, and was tired of picking up after him. Sometimes Obie regretted not (8) ***going out for football***, and instead being involved in something he could not discuss with his parents.

The chocolate sale had not been going well. Brother Leon said the boys had been infected by (9) ***apathy***. He blamed (10) ***Jerry***. He told Archie that if the sale was a failure, (11) ***The Vigils would go down the drain***. Archie then gave Jerry a new Assignment. He was told (12) ***to sell the chocolates.***

Jerry did not carry out his new Assignment. One day when he went to his locker, he saw that his poster (13) ***had been covered with paint or ink*** and his sneakers (14) ***had been shredded***. Another day he went to art class and discovered (15) ***the watercolor he had turned in was missing***. The punishment was truly turning out to be worse than the Assignment.

IV. Essay

Answers will vary, depending on classroom discussion.

V. <u>Vocabulary Part 1</u>

    Teacher: Choose ten words from the list and use them here.

	WORD	DEFINITION
1.	_____	_____
2.	_____	_____
3.	_____	_____
4.	_____	_____
5.	_____	_____
6.	_____	_____
7.	_____	_____
8.	_____	_____
9.	_____	_____
10.	_____	_____

V. <u>Vocabulary Part 2</u>

    Place the letter of the matching definition on the blank line.

A	1.	TUMULTUOUS	A.	riotous; chaotic
H	2.	SUPERIMPOSE	B.	downfall; antagonist
D	3.	RETALIATION	C.	difference; abnormality
J	4.	REBUKE	D.	revenge
C	5.	PERVERSION	E.	faintness
F	6.	PARODY	F.	imitation; take-off
G	7.	OBLIVION	G.	blackness; nothingness
B	8.	NEMESIS	H.	to lay on something else
I	9.	METICULOUS	I.	painstaking; precise
E	10.	LASSITUDE	J.	scolding

Advanced Short Answer Unit Test *The Chocolate War*

I. Matching/Identify

    1. BEAUTIFUL   A. painted over in Jerry's locker
    2. POSTER   B. pummeled Jerry
    3. FINE   C. New England boy's school
    4. SNEAKERS   D. accused of cheating by Leon
    5. TRINITY   E. The Vigils shredded Jerry's
    6. UNIVERSE   F. Jerry questioned whether or not to disturb it
    7. GREG BAILEY   G. assigned to dismantle a classroom
    8. JOHN CARTER   H. Mr. Renault's favorite word
    9. ROLAND GOUBERT   I. Archie's expression
   10. EMILE JANZA   J. president of The Vigils

II. Short Answer

1. Summarize the incident in class between Brother Leon and Bailey.

2. Who are The Vigils? Who are the key members/officers? What is an "Assignment"?

Advanced Short Answer Unit Test *The Chocolate War*

3. Describe the raffle and the fight. What went wrong with the fight? What happened to Jerry? What happened to Archie?

4. What are the main conflicts in the story? Are they resolved? If so, how? If not, why not?

5. What does the hippie in Chapter 1 represent?

III. Quotations

Discuss the significance of the following quotations.

1. "I know that, Archie. But Trinity is special, isn't it? If I didn't think the boys of Trinity could do it, do you think I would take a risk? Aren't we capable of what others aren't?" (Ch. 4)

Advanced Short Answer Unit Test *The Chocolate War*

2. "No."

3. "Look, Jerry. There's something rotten in that school. More than rotten . . . Evil." (Ch. 23)

4. "You see, Carter, people are two things: greedy and cruel. So we have a perfect set-up here. The greed part--a kid pays a buck for a chance to win a hundred. Plus fifty boxes of chocolates. The cruel part--watching two guys hitting each other, maybe hurting each other, while they're safe in the bleachers. That's why it works, Carter, because we're all bastards." (Ch. 36)

5. "Someday, Archie, you'll get yours." (Ch. 39)

Advanced Short Answer Unit Test *The Chocolate War*

IV. Vocabulary

Listen to the words and write them down. After you have written down all of the words, write a paragraph in which you use all of the words. The paragraph must in some way relate to *The Chocolate War*.

1.   6.
2.   7.
3.   8.
4.   9.
5.   10.

Multiple Choice Unit Test 1 *The Chocolate War*

I. <u>Matching/Identify</u>

    1.   ROLAND GOUBERT   A.   "A" student blackmailed by Leon
    2.   ARCHIE   B.   Archie's straight man
    3.   BROTHER LEON   C.   New England boy's school
    4.   DAVID CARONI   D.   author
    5.   EMILE JANZA   E.   was assigned to dismantle a classroom
    6.   ROBERT CORMIER   F.   president of The Vigils
    7.   TRINITY   G.   turned the prank back on The Vigils
    8.   JOHN CARTER   H.   pummeled Jerry
    9.   BROTHER JACQUES   I.   temporary Headmaster
    10.   OBIE   J.   Vigil assigner

II. <u>Multiple Choice</u>

1.   True or False: An Assignment was given to every freshman entering Trinity.
    A.   True
    B.   False

2.   The black box contains
    A.   twelve blue marbles and one yellow cat's eye marble.
    B.   red and white marbles.
    C.   one black and some white marbles.
    D.   equal number of green and orange marbles.

3.   Brother Leon told the boys they had turned the classroom into
    A.   Dante's Inferno.
    B.   the Inquisition.
    C.   Nazi Germany.
    D.   Orwell's 1984.

4.   Did the incident in Room 19 occur before or after the chocolate sale started?
    A.   It happened before the sale started.
    B.   It happened after the sale started.

5.   What was Jerry's response when Brother Leon asked him if he would sell the chocolates"
    A.   He said, "Yes."
    B.   He said, "No."

6. What was the irony about Archie's picture of Emile?
   A. Archie had already destroyed the picture.
   B. It was a picture of someone else.
   C. Archie had already posted it on the bulletin board.
   D. There had never been a picture.

7. Jerry learned where the secret of Brother Leon lurked. Where was it?
   A. It was locked away in a safe deposit box.
   B. It was in his eyes.
   C. It was in his prayer book
   D. It was in his handshake.

8. Who told Archie that Jerry was defying The Vigils by refusing to sell the chocolates?
   A. Brother Leon
   B. Goober
   C. Brother Eugene
   D. Obie

9. Which of the following did **not** happen to Jerry?
   A. He was hit from behind in the kidneys during football practice.
   B. The poster in his locker had been smeared with paint
   C. His new sneakers had been replaced with a pair of pink girl's sneakers
   D. His watercolor for art class was missing.

10. What happened to Jerry at the end of the story?
    A. He was taken away in an ambulance.
    B. He died in the stadium.
    C. He walked away, triumphant.
    D. Goober drove him home.

III. Quotations

Match the quotation and the missing word or phrase.

1. "The Vigils _____."
2. "And here's what you do, Goober. _____ ."
3. It's not The Vigils, Goob. _____."
4. "Your watercolor. The landscape assignment. _____."
5. "Know what, _____? You're a bright boy. You're cool. You catch on fast."
6. "_____ sold his fifty boxes."
7. "_____ Show them what you think of their goddam chocolates?"
8. It's a laugh, Goober, a fake. _____."
9. "Someday, _____, you'll get yours."
___ 10. "Hiding what? From whom?" "From everybody. From yourself, even. Hiding that deep, dark secret." "What secret?"

A. They're not in it anymore. It's me
B. Cochran
C. Don't disturb the universe, Goober, no matter what the posters say
D. Archie
E. will help
F. That you're a fairy. A queer. Living in the closet, hiding away."
G. You loosen
H. Today's the final day for handing it in. I don't find yours here
I. Goober
J. Wanna get even, Renault? Strike back? Get revenge?

Multiple Choice Unit Test 1 *The Chocolate War*

IV. Vocabulary Part 1
   Place the letter of the matching definition on the blank line.
   1. APATHY   A. slackers; shirkers
   2. CAMARADERIE   B. underhandedly
   3. DERISION   C. extremely painful
   4. EXCRUCIATING   D. indifference
   5. MUTINIED   E. quality
   6. MALINGERERS   F. revolted
   7. RAUCOUS   G. fearless; bold
   8. SURREPTITIOUSLY   H. companionship; friendship
   9. UNINTIMIDATED   I. loud; harsh
   10. CALIBER   J. ridicule; mocking

Vocabulary Part 2   Circle the letter next to the word that matches the definition.

11. **riotous; chaotic**
    a. caliber
    b. anguish
    c. **tumultuous**
    d. perennial

12. **differences; contradictions**
    a. **discrepancies**
    b. raucous
    c. futile
    d. nemesis

13. **destroying**
    a. shroud
    b. ingratiating
    c. fastidious
    d. **annihilating**

14. **irreverent; profane**
    a. **sacrilegious**
    b. resonance
    c. dissolution
    d. venomous

15. **ringing; resounding**
    a. eloquent
    b. **resonance**
    c. oblivion
    d. caliber

16. **scolding**
    a. conspiracy
    b. **rebuke**
    c. edifice
    d. audacity

17. **well-known**
    a. sacrilegious
    b. insolent
    c. oblivion
    d. **notorious**

18. **persnickety; particular**
    a. buoyant
    b. **fastidious**
    c. lassitude
    d. rancid

19. **cruel; brutal**
    a. **vicious**
    b. litany
    c. brandishing
    d. derision

20. **painstaking; precise**
    a. corrupt
    b. nemesis
    c. **meticulous**
    d. perusals

Multiple Choice Unit Test 2 *The Chocolate War*

I. <u>Matching/ Identify</u>

1. BEAUTIFUL   A. painted over in Jerry's locker
2. POSTER   B. pummeled Jerry
3. FINE   C. New England boy's school
4. SNEAKERS   D. accused of cheating by Leon
5. TRINITY   E. The Vigils shredded Jerry's
6. UNIVERSE   F. Jerry questioned whether or not to disturb it
7. GREG BAILEY   G. assigned to dismantle a classroom
8. JOHN CARTER   H. Mr. Renault's favorite word
9. ROLAND GOUBERT   I. Archie's expression
10. EMILE JANZA   J. president of The Vigils

II. <u>Multiple Choice</u>

1. Obie is
    A. the secretary to The Vigils and Archie's stooge.
    B. fired from his job for being late one last time.
    C. overjoyed at the attention Archie gives him.
    D. the Assigner for The Vigils.

2. During football practice Archie notices Renault's
    A. bloody nose.
    B. submission to the coach.
    C. toughness and stubbornness.
    D. lack of coordination.

3. True or False: Brother Leon is the Chairman of the Board at Trinity.
    A. True
    B. False

4. Brother Leon told the boys they had turned the classroom into
    A. Dante's Inferno.
    B. the Inquisition.
    C. Nazi Germany.
    D. Orwell's 1984.

Multiple Choice Unit Test 2 *The Chocolate War*

5. Which of these did **not** happen in Room 19?
    A. The author compared it to someone dropping The Bomb.
    B. It took 37 seconds for all of the furniture to collapse.
    C. Brother Eugene was crushed when the bookcase fell on top of him.
    D. Archie watched from the hallway.

6. On the day after Jerry's Assignment ended, Brother Leon called the roll for the chocolate sale. What did Jerry say when Brother Leon called his name?
    A. He said that he would not sell the chocolates.
    B. He said he would sell the chocolates.

7. What were the words on the poster in Jerry's locker?
    A. *Do not go harshly into that good night.*
    B. *He marches to the tune of a different drummer.*
    C. *Do I dare disturb the universe?*
    D. *To thine own self be true.*

8. What was Brother Leon's explanation for the way the sales were?
    A. He said The Vigils were not helping enough.
    B. He said the parents were not supportive.
    C. He said the boys had been infected by Jerry's apathy.
    D. He said the boys did not understand the importance of the sale.

9. Which of the following did **not** happen to Jerry? (Chapter 28)
    A. He was hit from behind in the kidneys during football practice.
    B. The poster in his locker had been smeared with paint
    C. His new sneakers had been replaced with a pair of pink girl's sneakers
    D. His watercolor for art class was missing.

10. What happened to Jerry at the end of the story?
    A. He was taken away in an ambulance.
    B. He died in the stadium.
    C. He walked away, triumphant.
    D. Goober drove him home.

Extra Credit: Draw a picture of one scene from the novel. Write a caption for the picture.

Multiple Choice Unit Test 2 *The Chocolate War*

III. Quotations

   Match the quotation with its missing word or phrase.

1. "These goddam assignments. _____"

2. "_____, why do you find it necessary to cheat?

3. "Tell you what, _____. At the end of the term, when the marks close, I'll review that particular test. Perhaps I'll be fresher then. Perhaps I'll see merit that wasn't apparent before. . . ."

4. "At this period of history, _____"

5. "He was supposed to start selling after the Assignment was over. So, now he's defying The Vigils. _____"

6. "I'll make it clear to you, Archie. _____"

7. "Welcome, _____. I imagine you are the villain here, aren't' you?"

8. "You really didn't use your best judgement tonight, Archie. _____"

9. "Look, _____. There's something rotten in that school. More than rotten . . . Evil."

10. It's not The Vigils, Goob. _____"

A. Caroni
B. man began to learn more about his environment--
C. But I realize you did it for the school. For Trinity."
D. If the sale goes down the drain, you and The Vigils also go down the drain. Believe me.
E. Jerry
F. Archie
G. Do they think it's easy? And the black box.
H. They're not in it anymore. It's me.
I. And a lot of guys know that. We are involved, Archie, whether we want to be or not."
J. Bailey

Multiple Choice Unit Test 2 *The Chocolate War*

IV. <u>Vocabulary Part 1</u> Place the letter of the matching definition on the blank line.

1. TUMULTUOUS
2. SUPERIMPOSE
3. BUOYANT
4. REBUKE
5. ELOQUENT
6. PARODY
7. OBLIVION
8. NEMESIS
9. ANNIHILATING
10. LASSITUDE

A. riotous; chaotic
B. downfall; antagonist
C. articulate; well-spoken
D. enthusiastic
E. faintness
F. imitation; take-off
G. blackness; nothingness
H. to lay on something else
I. destroying
J. scolding

<u>Vocabulary Part 2</u> Circle the letter next to the word that matches the definition.

11. **irreverent; profane**
    a. **sacrilegious**
    b. resonance
    c. dissolution
    d. venomous

12. **ringing; resounding**
    a. eloquent
    b. **resonance**
    c. oblivion
    d. caliber

13. **divested; stripped**
    a. superimpose
    b. **disembodied**
    c. insolent
    d. unintimidated

14. **difference; abnormality**
    a. adulation
    b. notorious
    c. **perversion**
    d. rancid

15. **fearless; bold**
    a. sacrilegious
    b. languidly
    c. **unintimidated**
    d. disembodied

16. **cruel; brutal**
    a. **vicious**
    b. litany
    c. brandishing
    d. derision

17. **painstaking; precise**
    a. corrupt
    b. nemesis
    c. **meticulous**
    d. perusals

18. **revenge**
    a. pandemonium
    b. desecrated
    c. malice
    d. **retaliation**

19. **self-righteously**
    a. excruciating
    b. **sanctimoniously**
    c. surreptitiously
    d. maliciously

20. **breaking up**
    a. **dissolution**
    b. crucifixes
    c. ingratiating
    d. resonance

ANSWER SHEET   Multiple Choice Unit Tests *The Chocolate War*

I. Matching	III. Quotations	IV. Vocabulary
1.	1.	1.
2.	2.	2.
3.	3.	3.
4.	4.	4.
5.	5.	5.
6.	6.	6.
7.	7.	7.
8.	8.	8.
9.	9.	9.
10.	10.	10.
		11.
		12.
		13.
		14.
		15.
		16.
		17.
		18.
		19.
		20.

II. Multiple Choice
1. (A) (B) (C) (D)
2. (A) (B) (C) (D)
3. (A) (B) (C) (D)
4. (A) (B) (C) (D)
5. (A) (B) (C) (D)
6. (A) (B) (C) (D)
7. (A) (B) (C) (D)
8. (A) (B) (C) (D)
9. (A) (B) (C) (D)
10. (A) (B) (C) (D)

ANSWER SHEET KEY   Multiple Choice Unit Test 1 *The Chocolate War*

To make an overlay, make a copy of this page, cut out the columns next to the answers for the matching and vocabulary sections, and take a hole punch and punch out the empty ( ) for the multiple choice section.

I. Matching
1. E
2. J
3. I
4. A
5. H
6. D
7. C
8. F
9. G
10. B

II. Multiple Choice
1. (A) ( ) (C) (D)
2. (A) (B) ( ) (D)
3. (A) (B) ( ) (D)
4. ( ) (B) (C) (D)
5. (A) ( ) (C) (D)
6. (A) (B) (C) ( )
7. (A) ( ) (C) (D)
8. (A) (B) (C) ( )
9. (A) (B) ( ) (D)
10. ( ) (B) (C) (D)

III. Quotations
1. E
2. G
3. A
4. H
5. B
6. I
7. J
8. C
9. D
10. F

IV. Vocabulary
1. D
2. H
3. J
4. C
5. F
6. A
7. I
8. B
9. G
10. E
11. C
12. A
13. D
14. A
15. A
16. B
17. D
18. B
19. A
20. C

ANSWER SHEET KEY   Multiple Choice Unit Test 2 *The Chocolate War*

I. Matching		III. Quotations		IV. Vocabulary	
1.	I	1.	G	1.	A
2.	A	2.	J	2.	H
3.	H	3.	A	3.	D
4.	E	4.	B	4.	J
5.	C	5.	I	5.	C
6.	F	6.	D	6.	F
7.	D	7.	F	7.	G
8.	J	8.	C	8.	B
9.	G	9.	E	9.	I
10.	B	10.	H	10.	E
				11.	A
				12.	B
				13.	B
				14.	C
				15.	C
				16.	A
				17.	C
				18.	D
				19.	B
				20.	A

II. Multiple Choice
1. ( )   (B)   (C)   (D)
2. (A)   (B)   ( )   (D)
3. (A)   ( )   (C)   (D)
4. (A)   (B)   ( )   (D)
5. (A)   (B)   ( )   (D)
6. ( )   (B)   (C)   (D)
7. (A)   (B)   ( )   (D)
8. (A)   (B)   ( )   (D)
9. (A)   (B)   ( )   (D)
10. ( )   (B)   (C)   (D)

UNIT RESOURCES

BULLETIN BOARD IDEAS *The Chocolate War*

1. Save one corner of the board for the best of students' *Chocolate War* writing assignments. You may want to use background maps of New England to represent the setting of the novel.

2. Take one of the word search puzzles from the resource section and with a marker copy it over in a large size on the bulletin board. Write the clue words to find to one side. Invite students prior to and after class to find the words and circle them on the bulletin board.

3. Copy and illustrate several of the quotations from the story.

4. Invite students to help make an interactive bulletin board quiz. Give each student a half sheet of paper folded in half so it can open like a little book. On the outside flap, have each student write a description of one of the characters in the text. On the inside, they will write the name of the character. You can staple or tack these papers to the bulletin board so students can read the descriptions and lift the flaps to find the answers.

5. Collect pictures of the New England area, especially of private schools there.

6. Have each student write and post a slogan or advertisement to use for selling chocolate.

7. Have students bring in (clean!) wrappers from their favorite candy bars glued to a page with a short poem or a few sentences about when they eat it, why they like it, etc.

8. Display articles about Robert Cormier and reviews of his books.

9. Have students design postcards depicting scenes in the book and use those for your bulletin board.

EXTRA ACTIVITIES - *The Chocolate War*

One of the difficulties in teaching a novel is that all students don't read at the same speed. One student who likes to read may take the book home and finish it in a day or two. Sometimes a few students finish the in-class assignments early. The problem, then, is finding suitable extra activities for students.

One thing that helps is to keep a little library of books and magazines related to the novel in the classroom. For this unit, you might check out other books by Robert Cormeir. A biography of the author would be interesting for some students. There are also many books with peer pressure as a theme that students might enjoy reading. Several journals have critiques of Robert Cormeir's works. Some of the students may enjoy reading these and responding either in writing or in discussion groups.

Other things you may keep on hand are puzzles and worksheets. Several of these relating to *Chocolate War* are included in this unit. Feel free to duplicate them for your class.

Some students may like to draw. You might devise a contest or allow some extra-credit grade for students who draw characters or scenes from this novel. Note, too, that if the students do not want to keep their drawings, you may pick up some extra bulletin board materials this way. If you have a contest and supply a prize, you could, possible make the drawing itself a non-refundable entry fee.

The pages which follow contain games, puzzles and worksheets. There are two main groups of activities: one group for the unit words (that is, words generally relating to the content of the text) and another group of activities for the vocabulary words.

The object here is to provide you with some extra materials you may use in any way you choose.

WORD SEARCH *The Chocolate War*

```
F I N E P H A R M A C I S T T R S E Y M
A B L Z K K E Z G S V D W R A E L I S J
T O G C F T G T F M N S R W Y I M H R T
H X S J R D K G E D W E T E M R J C X V
E I R A B Y E H S R E H A E J E R R Y G
R N C J J D T L R Q N P R K T I F A E W
A G B O B S I E E J U V H A E M D R I Y
M M L H R G M U V D N A L O R R G L B G
B A A N I F O G I L Z O R E E O S U O X
U T C V A O T E N H C Q C T P C B F L L
L C K J N O H N U O S N P G E N T I E V
A H B J J T E E H Q A A P S C R D T O J
N B O H H B R C N C H X Q O I H B U N N
C Q X R M A Z J G C K Q Y N S Q J A L N
E N A Z I L P R O B A T I O N T K E C V
B W G O A L P O S T S T R D T C E B Y K
S Q U A R E B O Y X Y D A V I D L R B J
```

AMBULANCE	CHAPTER	FINE	MOTHER	SNEAKERS
ARCHIE	CHOCOLATE	FOOTBALL	NAZI	SQUARE BOY
BEAUTIFUL	CORMIER	GOAL POSTS	OBIE	TRINITY
BLACK BOX	DAVID	GREG	PHARMACIST	UNIVERSE
BOXING MATCH	EMILE	HERSHEY BAR	POSTER	VIGILS
BRIAN	EUGENE	JERRY	PROBATION	WAR
CANCER	EYES	JOHN	QUARTERBACK	
CARTER	FATHER	LEON	ROLAND	

CROSSWORD *Chocolate War*

CROSSWORD CLUES *Chocolate War*

ACROSS
3 Archie's expression
8 Vigil assigner
10 Pummeled Jerry: ___ Janza
13 Dollar price of each box of chocolates
14 New England boys' school
16 Refused to sell the chocolates when his assignment was over
19 Archie's straight man
23 Jerry's passion
26 Leon calls class an example of ___ Germany
27 President of The Vigils
28 Brother ___; traumatized by The Vigils' prank
29 Harassment to Renault home
31 The Vigils shredded Jerry's
32 Hippie called Jerry "___ Boy"
33 She died of cancer
34 Jerry questioned whether or not to disturb it

DOWN
1 Jerry's mom died of this
2 Number of boxes of chocolates for each boy to sell
3 Result of raffle: ___ match
4 Number of thousands of boxes of candy Leon bought
5 Jerry thought his did not have an exciting life
6 Brother ___; temporary Headmaster
7 Brother Eugene's room number
9 Author
11 Key word in Brother Jacque's Vigil prank
12 Mr. Renault's favorite word
15 Archie's craving: ___ bar
17 Jerry was set up
18 ___ Goubert was assigned to dismantle a classroom
20 Archie's nemesis: black ___
21 These posts looked like crucifixes to Obie
22 Blackmailed by Leon: ___ Caroni
24 Candy sale tabulator: ___ Cochran
25 Trinity's secret society
27 Brother ___; turned the prank back on The Vigils after a clue from Archie
29 Painted over in Jerry's locker
30 Only one of them in black box: black ___

CROSSWORD ANSWER KEY *Chocolate War*

MATCHING QUIZ/WORKSHEET 1 - Chocolate War

___ 1. BOX   A. Jerry's passion

___ 2. GOAL   B. Pummeled Jerry: ___ Janza

___ 3. POSTER   C. ___ Goubert was assigned to dismantle a classroom

___ 4. PHARMACIST   D. Blackmailed by Leon: ___ Caroni

___ 5. ENVIRONMENT   E. Key word in Brother Jacque's Vigil prank

___ 6. JERRY   F. Hippie called Jerry ___ Boy

___ 7. SLEEPWALKING   G. Jerry thought his did not have an exciting life

___ 8. HERSHEY   H. Jerry questioned whether or not to disturb it

___ 9. ARCHIE   I. Archie's nemesis: black ___

___ 10. UNIVERSE   J. These posts looked like crucifixes to Obie

___ 11. MOTHER   K. Mr. Renault's favorite word

___ 12. FIFTY   L. Painted over in Jerry's locker

___ 13. SQUARE   M. Vigil assigner

___ 14. EMILE   N. Number of boxes of chocolates for each boy to sell

___ 15. CANCER   O. Jerry's mom died of this

___ 16. DAVID   P. How Jerry sees his father's living

___ 17. FATHER   Q. She died of cancer

___ 18. BOXING   R. Brother ___; temporary Headmaster

___ 19. ROLAND   S. Leon calls class an example of ___ Germany

___ 20. TWO   T. Carter threatened Archie with this

___ 21. FINE   U. Refused to sell the chocolates when his assignment was over

___ 22. NAZI   V. Archie's craving: ___ bar

___ 23. LEON   W. Dollar price of each box of chocolates

___ 24. PROBATION   X. Result of raffle: ___ match

___ 25. FOOTBALL   Y. Mr. Renault's occupation

KEY: MATCHING QUIZ/WORKSHEET 1 - Chocolate War

I -	1. BOX	A.	Jerry's passion
J -	2. GOAL	B.	Pummeled Jerry: ___ Janza
L -	3. POSTER	C.	___ Goubert was assigned to dismantle a classroom
Y -	4. PHARMACIST	D.	Blackmailed by Leon: ___ Caroni
E -	5. ENVIRONMENT	E.	Key word in Brother Jacque's Vigil prank
U -	6. JERRY	F.	Hippie called Jerry ___ Boy
P -	7. SLEEPWALKING	G.	Jerry thought his did not have an exciting life
V -	8. HERSHEY	H.	Jerry questioned whether or not to disturb it
M -	9. ARCHIE	I.	Archie's nemesis: black ___
H -	10. UNIVERSE	J.	These posts looked like crucifixes to Obie
Q -	11. MOTHER	K.	Mr. Renault's favorite word
N -	12. FIFTY	L.	Painted over in Jerry's locker
F -	13. SQUARE	M.	Vigil assigner
B -	14. EMILE	N.	Number of boxes of chocolates for each boy to sell
O -	15. CANCER	O.	Jerry's mom died of this
D -	16. DAVID	P.	How Jerry sees his father's living
G -	17. FATHER	Q.	She died of cancer
X -	18. BOXING	R.	Brother ___; temporary Headmaster
C -	19. ROLAND	S.	Leon calls class an example of ___ Germany
W	20. TWO	T.	Carter threatened Archie with this
K -	21. FINE	U.	Refused to sell the chocolates when his assignment was over
S -	22. NAZI	V.	Archie's craving: ___ bar
R -	23. LEON	W.	Dollar price of each box of chocolates
T -	24. PROBATION	X.	Result of raffle: ___ match
A -	25. FOOTBALL	Y.	Mr. Renault's occupation

MATCHING QUIZ/WORKSHEET 2 - Chocolate War

___ 1. HERSHEY   A. President of The Vigils
___ 2. RAFFLE   B. Pummeled Jerry: ___ Janza
___ 3. DAVID   C. Result of raffle: ___ match
___ 4. GOAL   D. Jerry's passion
___ 5. QUARTERBACK   E. Refused to sell the chocolates when his assignment was over
___ 6. LEON   F. Vigil assigner
___ 7. FOOTBALL   G. Used to dismantle Brother Eugene's room
___ 8. NAZI   H. Number of thousands of boxes of candy Leon bought
___ 9. POSTER   I. Brother ___; traumatized by The Vigils' prank
___ 10. TWENTY   J. Carter threatened Archie with this
___ 11. SLEEPWALKING K. Jerry was set up
___ 12. TRINITY   L. Painted over in Jerry's locker
___ 13. SCREWDRIVERS M. New England boys' school
___ 14. JERRY   N. Brother ___; temporary Headmaster
___ 15. UNIVERSE   O. Leon calls class an example of ___ Germany
___ 16. PROBATION   P. How Jerry sees his father's living
___ 17. EMILE   Q. These posts looked like crucifixes to Obie
___ 18. SNEAKERS   R. Jerry's football position
___ 19. BEAUTIFUL   S. Blackmailed by Leon: ___ Caroni
___ 20. ARCHIE   T. ___ Goubert was assigned to dismantle a classroom
___ 21. JOHN   U. Archie's craving: ___ bar
___ 22. EUGENE   V. Jerry questioned whether or not to disturb it
___ 23. MOTHER   W. Archie's expression
___ 24. ROLAND   X. The Vigils shredded Jerry's
___ 25. BOXING   Y. She died of cancer

KEY: MATCHING QUIZ/WORKSHEET 2 - Chocolate War

U - 1.	HERSHEY	A. President of The Vigils
K - 2.	RAFFLE	B. Pummeled Jerry: ___ Janza
S - 3.	DAVID	C. Result of raffle: ___ match
Q - 4.	GOAL	D. Jerry's passion
R - 5.	QUARTERBACK	E. Refused to sell the chocolates when his assignment was over
N - 6.	LEON	F. Vigil assigner
D - 7.	FOOTBALL	G. Used to dismantle Brother Eugene's room
O - 8.	NAZI	H. Number of thousands of boxes of candy Leon bought
L - 9.	POSTER	I. Brother ___; traumatized by The Vigils' prank
H - 10.	TWENTY	J. Carter threatened Archie with this
P - 11.	SLEEPWALKING	K. Jerry was set up
M - 12.	TRINITY	L. Painted over in Jerry's locker
G - 13.	SCREWDRIVERS	M. New England boys' school
E - 14.	JERRY	N. Brother ___; temporary Headmaster
V - 15.	UNIVERSE	O. Leon calls class an example of ___ Germany
J - 16.	PROBATION	P. How Jerry sees his father's living
B - 17.	EMILE	Q. These posts looked like crucifixes to Obie
X - 18.	SNEAKERS	R. Jerry's football position
W - 19.	BEAUTIFUL	S. Blackmailed by Leon: ___ Caroni
F - 20.	ARCHIE	T. ___ Goubert was assigned to dismantle a classroom
A - 21.	JOHN	U. Archie's craving: ___ bar
I - 22.	EUGENE	V. Jerry questioned whether or not to disturb it
Y - 23.	MOTHER	W. Archie's expression
T - 24.	ROLAND	X. The Vigils shredded Jerry's
C - 25.	BOXING	Y. She died of cancer

JUGGLE LETTER REVIEW GAME CLUE SHEET - Chocolate War

1. OJNH = 1. _____
President of The Vigils

2. HRPISACAMT = 2. _____
Mr. Renault's occupation

3. BOEI = 3. _____
Archie's straight man

4. MCROEIR = 4. _____
Author

5. ECCANR = 5. _____
Jerry's mom died of this

6. EIGKASELNPWL = 6. _____
How Jerry sees his father's living

7. OENL = 7. _____
Brother ___; temporary Headmaster

8. VEIRSNUE = 8. _____
Jerry questioned whether or not to disturb it

9. HPEON = 9. _____
Harassment to Renault home

10. AOLG =10. _____
These posts looked like crucifixes to Obie

11. EIELM =11. _____
Pummeled Jerry: ___ Janza

12. OOLTALFB =12. _____
Jerry's passion

13. BATONPIRO =13. _____
Carter threatened Archie with this

14. ENMIOENTVRN =14. _____
Key word in Brother Jacque's Vigil prank

15. GVSIIL =15. _____
Trinity's secret society

16. LFRFAE =16. _____
Jerry was set up

17. ARURKECAQTB =17. _____
Jerry's football position

18. ITFFY =18. _____
Number of boxes of chocolates for each boy to sell

19. IEFN =19. _____
Mr. Renault's favorite word

20. LEAMRB =20. _____
Only one of them in black box: black ___

21. DNAROL =21. _____
___ Goubert was assigned to dismantle a classroom

22. NTRITIY =22. _____
New England boys' school

23. UGEENE =23. _____
Brother ___; traumatized by The Vigils' prank

24. ARSQEU =24. _____
Hippie called Jerry ___ Boy

25. YHSHERE =25. _____
Archie's craving: ___ bar

26. TMERHO =26. _____
She died of cancer

27. IDVAD =27. _____
Blackmailed by Leon: ___ Caroni

28. QSACEJU =28. _____
Brother ___; turned the prank back on The Vigils after a clue from Archie

29. NBARI =29. _____
Candy sale tabulator: ___ Cochran

30. INEETNNE =30. _____
Brother Eugene's room number

31. NIAZ   =31. _____
                    Leon calls class an example of ___ Germany

32. OTW   =32. _____
                    Dollar price of each box of chocolates

33. IFUEATUBL   =33. _____
                    Archie's expression

34. EJYRR   =34. _____
                    Refused to sell the chocolates when his assignment was over

35. HAERFT   =35. _____
                    Jerry thought his did not have an exciting life

36. ERCWRSSIVRDE   =36. _____
                    Used to dismantle Brother Eugene's room

37. REAHCI   =37. _____
                    Vigil assigner

38. GIXBON   =38. _____
                    Result of raffle: ___ match

KEY: JUGGLE LETTER REVIEW GAME CLUE SHEET - Chocolate War

1. OJNH = 1. JOHN
   President of The Vigils

2. HRPISACAMT = 2. PHARMACIST
   Mr. Renault's occupation

3. BOEI = 3. OBIE
   Archie's straight man

4. MCROEIR = 4. CORMIER
   Author

5. ECCANR = 5. CANCER
   Jerry's mom died of this

6. EIGKASELNPWL = 6. SLEEPWALKING
   How Jerry sees his father's living

7. OENL = 7. LEON
   Brother ___; temporary Headmaster

8. VEIRSNUE = 8. UNIVERSE
   Jerry questioned whether or not to disturb it

9. HPEON = 9. PHONE
   Harassment to Renault home

10. AOLG = 10. GOAL
    These posts looked like crucifixes to Obie

11. EIELM = 11. EMILE
    Pummeled Jerry: ___ Janza

12. OOLTALFB = 12. FOOTBALL
    Jerry's passion

13. BATONPIRO = 13. PROBATION
    Carter threatened Archie with this

14. ENMIOENTVRN = 14. ENVIRONMENT
    Key word in Brother Jacque's Vigil prank

15. GVSIIL = 15. VIGILS
    Trinity's secret society

16. LFRFAE =16. RAFFLE
Jerry was set up

17. ARURKECAQTB =17. QUARTERBACK
Jerry's football position

18. ITFFY =18. FIFTY
Number of boxes of chocolates for each boy to sell

19. IEFN =19. FINE
Mr. Renault's favorite word

20. LEAMRB =20. MARBLE
Only one of them in black box: black ___

21. DNAROL =21. ROLAND
___ Goubert was assigned to dismantle a classroom

22. NTRITIY =22. TRINITY
New England boys' school

23. UGEENE =23. EUGENE
Brother ___; traumatized by The Vigils' prank

24. ARSQEU =24. SQUARE
Hippie called Jerry ___ Boy

25. YHSHERE =25. HERSHEY
Archie's craving: ___ bar

26. TMERHO =26. MOTHER
She died of cancer

27. IDVAD =27. DAVID
Blackmailed by Leon: ___ Caroni

28. QSACEJU =28. JACQUES
Brother ___; turned the prank back on The Vigils after a clue from Archie

29. NBARI =29. BRIAN
Candy sale tabulator: ___ Cochran

30. INEETNNE =30. NINETEEN
Brother Eugene's room number

31. NIAZ =31. NAZI
Leon calls class an example of ___ Germany

32. OTW =32. TWO
Dollar price of each box of chocolates

33. IFUEATUBL =33. BEAUTIFUL
Archie's expression

34. EJYRR =34. JERRY
Refused to sell the chocolates when his assignment was over

35. HAERFT =35. FATHER
Jerry thought his did not have an exciting life

36. ERCWRSSIVRDE =36. SCREWDRIVERS
Used to dismantle Brother Eugene's room

37. REAHCI =37. ARCHIE
Vigil assigner

38. GIXBON =38. BOXING
Result of raffle: ___ match

VOCABULARY RESOURCE MATERIALS

VOCABULARY WORD SEARCH *The Chocolate War*

```
S U P E R I M P O S E R E B I L A C E M
U H K L D G M P T R O X E H R N P K P J
O D R N E I B A X B X F Q S N A U D P N
U N I O G X F C L P Q Q U I O B N S H L
T S O G U X U I Y I C H H T E N W C N Y
L E T A C D V L C W C I P R I F A J I N
U M O D N I M Y T E L E B S P L J N C D
M B R T O G N E W A R S E Y A A E O C F
U O I N I R U T T U N T Z N R I M I V E
T D O E T M N I S I U C G A O N O S I N
I I U U A E N A S B C U Y T D N R R C L
N E S Q L G L E I H I U P I Y E T E I G
I D S O U S V R M D X U L L J R A V O S
E S S L D S T T L E R Y K O G E L R U C
D N X E A T B Y X R S C Y V U P I E S W
I Y H T A P A N O I S I R E D S T P B H
B U O Y A N T C N D F F S G G Y Y N F J
```

ADULATION	CORRUPT	INSOLENT	NEMESIS	RANCID
ANGUISH	DERISION	LANGUIDLY	NOTORIOUS	REBUKE
ANNIHILATING	DISEMBODIED	LITANY	OBLIVION	RESONANCE
APATHY	EDIFICE	MALICE	PARODY	SHROUD
ATTRIBUTES	ELOQUENT	METICULOUS	PERENNIAL	SUPERIMPOSE
BUOYANT	EXULTANCY	MORTALITY	PERUSALS	TUMULTUOUS
CALIBER	FUTILE	MUTINIED	PERVERSION	VICIOUS

VOCABULARY CROSSWORD *Chocolate War*

VOCABULARY CROSSWORD CLUES *Chocolate War*

ACROSS
1 Violated; defiled
4 Readings
11 Cruel; brutal
12 Revenge
16 Grumblers; complainers
19 Revolted
24 Particular
25 Plot
26 Breaking up
27 Agony; grief

DOWN
2 Quality
3 Structure
4 Distrust; suspicion
5 Ringing; resounding
6 Cloak; graveclothes
7 Prayer
8 Divested; stripped
9 Secretly
10 Rank; offensive; spoiled
13 Faintness
14 Well-known for bad reasons
15 Qualities
16 Humanity
17 Downfall; antagonist
18 Extremely painful
19 Spite; ill-will
20 Wheedling
21 Painstaking; precise
22 Articulate; well-spoken
23 Imitation; take-off
24 Useless

VOCABULARY CROSSWORD ANSWER KEY *Chocolate War*

VOCABULARY WORKSHEET 1 - Chocolate War

___ 1. LANGUIDLY   A. Destroying

___ 2. EDIFICE   B. Violated; defiled

___ 3. CAMARADERIE   C. Grumblers; complainers

___ 4. CONSPIRACY   D. Cruel; brutal

___ 5. SANCTIMONIOUSLY   E. Irreversible

___ 6. VENOMOUS   F. Enduring; lasting

___ 7. DISEMBODIED   G. Structure

___ 8. EXULTANCY   H. Extremely painful

___ 9. ANNIHILATING   I. In a kind manner; with good will

___ 10. MALCONTENTS   J. Divested; stripped

___ 11. BENEVOLENTLY   K. Hurling; flinging

___ 12. EXEMPLIFIED   L. Joy; jubilation

___ 13. PANDEMONIUM   M. Companionship; friendship

___ 14. VICIOUS   N. Sassy; disrespectful

___ 15. PERENNIAL   O. Plot

___ 16. OBLIVION   P. Blackness; nothingness

___ 17. DESECRATED   Q. Represented; illustrated

___ 18. CALIBER   R. Qualities

___ 19. IRREVOCABLE   S. Differences; contradictions

___ 20. CATAPULTING   T. Poisonous

___ 21. INSOLENT   U. Breaking up

___ 22. DISSOLUTION   V. Quality

___ 23. ATTRIBUTES   W. Self-righteously

___ 24. DISCREPANCIES   X. With indifference

___ 25. EXCRUCIATING   Y. Chaos; disorder

KEY: VOCABULARY WORKSHEET 1- Chocolate War

X - 1.	LANGUIDLY	A. Destroying
G - 2.	EDIFICE	B. Violated; defiled
M - 3.	CAMARADERIE	C. Grumblers; complainers
O - 4.	CONSPIRACY	D. Cruel; brutal
W - 5.	SANCTIMONIOUSLY	E. Irreversible
T - 6.	VENOMOUS	F. Enduring; lasting
J - 7.	DISEMBODIED	G. Structure
L - 8.	EXULTANCY	H. Extremely painful
A - 9.	ANNIHILATING	I. In a kind manner; with good will
C - 10.	MALCONTENTS	J. Divested; stripped
I - 11.	BENEVOLENTLY	K. Hurling; flinging
Q - 12.	EXEMPLIFIED	L. Joy; jubilation
Y - 13.	PANDEMONIUM	M. Companionship; friendship
D - 14.	VICIOUS	N. Sassy; disrespectful
F - 15.	PERENNIAL	O. Plot
P - 16.	OBLIVION	P. Blackness; nothingness
B - 17.	DESECRATED	Q. Represented; illustrated
V - 18.	CALIBER	R. Qualities
E - 19.	IRREVOCABLE	S. Differences; contradictions
K - 20.	CATAPULTING	T. Poisonous
N - 21.	INSOLENT	U. Breaking up
U - 22.	DISSOLUTION	V. Quality
R - 23.	ATTRIBUTES	W. Self-righteously
S - 24.	DISCREPANCIES	X. With indifference
H - 25.	EXCRUCIATING	Y. Chaos; disorder

VOCABULARY WORKSHEET 2 - Chocolate War

___ 1. DERISION   A. Articulate; well-spoken
___ 2. RANCID   B. Irreversible
___ 3. APATHY   C. Revenge
___ 4. INGRATIATING   D. Enduring; lasting
___ 5. CORRUPT   E. Breaking up
___ 6. ADULATION   F. Rank; offensive; spoiled
___ 7. SUPERIMPOSE   G. Structure
___ 8. BUOYANT   H. Ringing; resounding
___ 9. IRREVOCABLE   I. Praise; worship
___ 10. ALTERATION   J. Waving
___ 11. OBLIVION   K. Demolished
___ 12. DISCREPANCIES   L. Differences; contradictions
___ 13. ELOQUENT   M. Wicked; dishonest
___ 14. ANGUISH   N. Difference; abnormality
___ 15. OBLITERATED   O. Enthusiastic
___ 16. EXCRUCIATING   P. Ridicule; mocking
___ 17. LITANY   Q. Qualities
___ 18. RETALIATION   R. To lay on or over something else
___ 19. EDIFICE   S. Prayer
___ 20. ATTRIBUTES   T. Extremely painful
___ 21. PERENNIAL   U. Indifference
___ 22. PERVERSION   V. Wheedling
___ 23. BRANDISHING   W. Agony; grief
___ 24. RESONANCE   X. Blackness; nothingness
___ 25. DISSOLUTION   Y. Change

KEY: VOCABULARY WORKSHEET 2 - Chocolate War

P - 1. DERISION	A.	Articulate; well-spoken
F - 2. RANCID	B.	Irreversible
U - 3. APATHY	C.	Revenge
V - 4. INGRATIATING	D.	Enduring; lasting
M - 5. CORRUPT	E.	Breaking up
I - 6. ADULATION	F.	Rank; offensive; spoiled
R - 7. SUPERIMPOSE	G.	Structure
O - 8. BUOYANT	H.	Ringing; resounding
B - 9. IRREVOCABLE	I.	Praise; worship
Y - 10. ALTERATION	J.	Waving
X - 11. OBLIVION	K.	Demolished
L - 12. DISCREPANCIES	L.	Differences; contradictions
A - 13. ELOQUENT	M.	Wicked; dishonest
W - 14. ANGUISH	N.	Difference; abnormality
K - 15. OBLITERATED	O.	Enthusiastic
T - 16. EXCRUCIATING	P.	Ridicule; mocking
S - 17. LITANY	Q.	Qualities
C - 18. RETALIATION	R.	To lay on or over something else
G - 19. EDIFICE	S.	Prayer
Q - 20. ATTRIBUTES	T.	Extremely painful
D - 21. PERENNIAL	U.	Indifference
N - 22. PERVERSION	V.	Wheedling
J - 23. BRANDISHING	W.	Agony; grief
H - 24. RESONANCE	X.	Blackness; nothingness
E - 25. DISSOLUTION	Y.	Change

VOCABULARY JUGGLE LETTER REVIEW GAME CLUE SHEET 1 - Chocolate War

1. TLNAIY = 1. _____
Prayer

2. SIDUTNOSIOL = 2. _____
Breaking up

3. SCAIPYNCRO = 3. _____
Plot

4. NLIUATTGAPC = 4. _____
Hurling; flinging

5. INNLRPEEA = 5. _____
Enduring; lasting

6. SNITBOHINII = 6. _____
Fears; misgivings

7. OEOMVUSN = 7. _____
Poisonous

8. VIRBAREOLCE = 8. _____
Irreversible

9. OYUNLSOSNCAMIIT = 9. _____
Self-righteously

10. CIUOIVS =10. _____
Cruel; brutal

11. VYUIRFLET =11. _____
Secretly

12. YTNAUBO =12. _____
Enthusiastic

13. RDEMICEARAA =13. _____
Companionship; friendship

14. OUNQETEL =14. _____
Articulate; well-spoken

15. LUOTMUUTS =15. _____
Riotous; chaotic

16. YIDLNUAGL   =16. _____
                             With indifference

17. SSAIIUDTFO   =17. _____
                             Particular

18. AEIMTNNUDIDIT   =18. _____
                             Fearless; bold

19. LAAETTONIR   =19. _____
                             Change

20. TCROPUR   =20. _____
                             Wicked; dishonest

21. ICDNAR   =21. _____
                             Rank; offensive; spoiled

22. ROIENRPESV   =22. _____
                             Difference; abnormality

23. AEOENNCRS   =23. _____
                             Ringing; resounding

24. ISRNSAEPDICEC   =24. _____
                             Differences; contradictions

25. HTAANGIINNIL   =25. _____
                             Destroying

26. OUNIADMMNEP   =26. _____
                             Chaos; disorder

27. YTEVNLEBNEOL   =27. _____
                             In a kind manner; with good will

28. UFEITL   =28. _____
                             Useless

29. AHBINSGRDNI   =29. _____
                             Waving

30. RPUTSSUILEYTORI   =30. _____
                             Underhandedly

KEY: VOCABULARY JUGGLE LETTER REVIEW GAME CLUE SHEET 1 - Chocolate War

1. TLNAIY = 1. LITANY
   Prayer

2. SIDUTNOSIOL = 2. DISSOLUTION
   Breaking up

3. SCAIPYNCRO = 3. CONSPIRACY
   Plot

4. NLIUATTGAPC = 4. CATAPULTING
   Hurling; flinging

5. INNLRPEEA = 5. PERENNIAL
   Enduring; lasting

6. SNITBOHINII = 6. INHIBITIONS
   Fears; misgivings

7. OEOMVUSN = 7. VENOMOUS
   Poisonous

8. VIRBAREOLCE = 8. IRREVOCABLE
   Irreversible

9. OYUNLSOSNCAMIIT = 9. SANCTIMONIOUSLY
   Self-righteously

10. CIUOIVS = 10. VICIOUS
    Cruel; brutal

11. VYUIRFLET = 11. FURTIVELY
    Secretly

12. YTNAUBO = 12. BUOYANT
    Enthusiastic

13. RDEMICEARAA = 13. CAMARADERIE
    Companionship; friendship

14. OUNQETEL = 14. ELOQUENT
    Articulate; well-spoken

15. LUOTMUUTS = 15. TUMULTUOUS
    Riotous; chaotic

16. YIDLNUAGL =16. LANGUIDLY
With indifference

17. SSAIIUDTFO =17. FASTIDIOUS
Particular

18. AEIMTNNUDIDIT =18. UNINTIMIDATED
Fearless; bold

19. LAAETTONIR =19. ALTERATION
Change

20. TCROPUR =20. CORRUPT
Wicked; dishonest

21. ICDNAR =21. RANCID
Rank; offensive; spoiled

22. ROIENRPESV =22. PERVERSION
Difference; abnormality

23. AEOENNCRS =23. RESONANCE
Ringing; resounding

24. ISRNSAEPDICEC =24. DISCREPANCIES
Differences; contradictions

25. HTAANGIINNIL =25. ANNIHILATING
Destroying

26. OUNIADMMNEP =26. PANDEMONIUM
Chaos; disorder

27. YTEVNLEBNEOL =27. BENEVOLENTLY
In a kind manner; with good will

28. UFEITL =28. FUTILE
Useless

29. AHBINSGRDNI =29. BRANDISHING
Waving

30. RPUTSSUILEYTORI =30. SURREPTITIOUSLY
Underhandedly

VOCABULARY JUGGLE LETTER REVIEW GAME CLUE SHEET 2 - Chocolate War

1. IINRSEOD = 1. _____
   Ridicule; mocking

2. NSONTLTMEAC = 2. _____
   Grumblers; complainers

3. SEMSNIE = 3. _____
   Downfall; antagonist

4. LICAME – 4. _____
   Spite; ill-will

5. ILRCEAB = 5. _____
   Quality

6. TAAHPY = 6. _____
   Indifference

7. MIPEOPRSSEU = 7. _____
   To lay on or over something else

8. TDCESRDEEA = 8. _____
   Violated; defiled

9. LOIAETRNATI = 9. _____
   Revenge

10. CAUYDATI =10. _____
    Daring; boldness

11. YLNUCAETX =11. _____
    Joy; jubilation

12. LCMITUEUOS =12. _____
    Painstaking; precise

13. ICEDIEF =13. _____
    Structure

14. UTNDIEMI =14. _____
    Revolted

15. EITUABRTST =15. _____
    Qualities

16. GIIIARNTNTAG =16. _____
Wheedling

17. APRONAAI =17. _____
Distrust; suspicion

18. IRSELISAOCGU =18. _____
Irreverent; profane

19. TLAESDISU =19. _____
Faintness

20. OOIINLVB =20. _____
Blackness; nothingness

21. SGAUHNI =21. _____
Agony; grief

22. IODEIDEBSMD =22. _____
Divested; stripped

23. NNTELSIO =23. _____
Sassy; disrespectful

24. UDSRHO =24. _____
Cloak; graveclothes

25. INRTSOUOO =25. _____
Well-known for bad reasons

26. UOLNAITDA =26. _____
Praise; worship

27. ELARUPSS =27. _____
Readings

28. ESFCCIIURX =28. _____
Crosses with the figure of Christ crucified on them

29. EILEDFXPEIM =29. _____
Represented; illustrated

30. EGMESALRNRI =30. _____
Slackers; shirkers

KEY: VOCABULARY JUGGLE LETTER REVIEW GAME CLUE SHEET 2 - Chocolate War

1. IINRSEOD = 1. DERISION
   Ridicule; mocking

2. NSONTLTMEAC = 2. MALCONTENTS
   Grumblers; complainers

3. SEMSNIE = 3. NEMESIS
   Downfall; antagonist

4. LICAME = 4. MALICE
   Spite; ill-will

5. ILRCEAB = 5. CALIBER
   Quality

6. TAAHPY = 6. APATHY
   Indifference

7. MIPEOPRSSEU = 7. SUPERIMPOSE
   To lay on or over something else

8. TDCESRDEEA = 8. DESECRATED
   Violated; defiled

9. LOIAETRNATI = 9. RETALIATION
   Revenge

10. CAUYDATI =10. AUDACITY
    Daring; boldness

11. YLNUCAETX =11. EXULTANCY
    Joy; jubilation

12. LCMITUEUOS =12. METICULOUS
    Painstaking; precise

13. ICEDIEF =13. EDIFICE
    Structure

14. UTNDIEMI =14. MUTINIED
    Revolted

15. EITUABRTST =15. ATTRIBUTES
    Qualities

16. GIIIARNTNTAG =16. INGRATIATING
Wheedling

17. APRONAAI =17. PARANOIA
Distrust; suspicion

18. IRSELISAOCGU =18. SACRILEGIOUS
Irreverent; profane

19. TLAESDISU =19. LASSITUDE
Faintness

20. OOIINLVB =20. OBLIVION
Blackness; nothingness

21. SGAUHNI =21. ANGUISH
Agony; grief

22. IODEIDEBSMD =22. DISEMBODIED
Divested; stripped

23. NNTELSIO =23. INSOLENT
Sassy; disrespectful

24. UDSRHO =24. SHROUD
Cloak; graveclothes

25. INRTSOUOO =25. NOTORIOUS
Well-known for bad reasons

26. UOLNAITDA =26. ADULATION
Praise; worship

27. ELARUPSS =27. PERUSALS
Readings

28. ESFCCIIURX =28. CRUCIFIXES
Crosses with the figure of Christ crucified on them

29. EILEDFXPEIM =29. EXEMPLIFIED
Represented; illustrated

30. EGMESALRNRI =30. MALINGERERS
Slackers; shirkers

www.ingramcontent.com/pod-product-compliance
Lightning Source LLC
LaVergne TN
LVHW081535060526
838200LV00048B/2089